Asking them Questions

Asking them Questions

A Selection from the Three Series

'They found Him . . . sitting in the
midst of the doctors, both hearing
them, and asking them questions.'
LUKE ii. 46

Edited by

RONALD SELBY WRIGHT

LONDON
OXFORD UNIVERSITY PRESS
NEW YORK   TORONTO

Oxford University Press, Ely House, London W. 1

GLASGOW NEW YORK TORONTO MELBOURNE WELLINGTON
CAPE TOWN SALISBURY IBADAN NAIROBI LUSAKA ADDIS ABABA
BOMBAY CALCUTTA MADRAS KARACHI LAHORE DACCA
KUALA LUMPUR HONG KONG TOKYO

FIRST EDITION 1953
REPRINTED 1955, 1960, 1963, AND 1967

PRINTED IN GREAT BRITAIN
AT THE UNIVERSITY PRESS, OXFORD
BY VIVIAN RIDLER
PRINTER TO THE UNIVERSITY

Note

MANY thousands of copies of *Asking Them Questions*, First, Second, and Third Series, have been printed, which would seem to show that these three books have been found useful and helpful during the seventeen years since the First Series appeared. It has seemed that the time had come to collect into one volume a selection of the articles that in the Editor's judgement would be found most valuable so that they may continue to be available in this handy form. It has been no easy task to make the selection and it has meant leaving out some of my favourite articles—that, for example, by Field-Marshal Slim on what he calls *the* virtue of courage, where he begins by saying 'I don't believe that there is any man who in his heart of hearts wouldn't rather be called brave than have any other virtue attributed to him'; or the article on Leadership by Brigadier Bernard Fergusson,[1] or the article by Fr. H. H. Kelly on the angels—and so much else; or . . . but why continue? Here after much thought is the selection seeking to cover as wide and comprehensive a field as possible in one volume. And in that I hope we have not been unsuccessful. Of the original one hundred and fourteen articles we have retained forty-three and none of these has been abridged or altered.

I should like to thank all who have so kindly advised me in my choice including Walter Oakeshott, Head Master of Winchester, Donald Crichton-Miller, Head Master of Fettes, and especially D. Forbes Mackintosh,

[1] I feel that it would be of interest to note here Bernard Fergusson's seven qualities that are invaluable in right leadership: i. knowledge of your job; ii. belief in your cause; iii. determination; iv. discipline; v. confidence; vi. foresight; vii. loyalty.

Headmaster of Loretto, R. W. Moore, Head Master of Harrow, A. Lionel F. Smith, sometime Rector of the Edinburgh Academy, and my colleague, the Rev. D. A. R. McGregor. And once more I am grateful for the help and encouragement of my friends J. P. Shaw and Harry Richmond.

As before, any profit from this book will go to help the work of Boys' Clubs.

RONALD SELBY WRIGHT

THE MANSE OF THE CANONGATE
EDINBURGH
Christmas, 1952

CHARLES LAING WARR

GEORGE FIELDEN MACLEOD

ANDREW NEVILE DAVIDSON

D.D.D.

Respice in servos Tuos, et in opera Tua:
et dirige filios eorum.
Et sit splendor DOMINI DEI *nostri super nos:*
et opera manuum nostrarum dirige super nos:
et opus manuum nostrarum dirige.

From the Preface to the First Series
(1935)

UNLIKE most books for boys, and for leaders, this one owes its genesis to the boys themselves, for it was from them that I learnt that one of the things a boy really needs is a right understanding of the Christian Faith.

This is how it happened. One night after our usual service in the Club Chapel, I handed to each boy a paper on which he was asked to write any question concerning the Christian Faith which perplexed him. These questions are in this book, every one of them actually asked by a member of our Club and Scout Troop, no one of whom was at the time over eighteen. The questions came to me as a revelation of just what boys are thinking. 'Fancy asking a question like that', I said, as I looked over the questions, 'so he does think about other things besides football and swimming.' A telegraph messenger asked 'What was Christ's position as God if He prayed to God?'; an apprentice plumber about the 'Second Coming'; a butcher's messenger boy about the Trinity; a young gardener about the Soul; one schoolboy about the Vision of God; another about our Lord as a boy; and so on. More than half the questions were about subjects like Heaven and Hell, evil, sin, and suffering (involving the extent of the power of God), and the relation of Jesus Christ to God.

I saw at once the mistake we in our Clubs, Brigade Companies, and Scout Groups so often make, of presenting to our boys a vague and sentimental watered-down religion, as if the Christian religion were *merely* 'living a decent life, keeping fit, helping others, and all that sort of thing. . . .' Then they grow up and leave us, the best of them resolving to be fit and to do their best. This, of course, is a good thing as far as it goes, and I am sure that it is pleasing in God's eyes. *As far as it goes*, but it appears to me now more than ever that it does not go far enough. I once heard Colonel Ronald B. Campbell say that missionaries of the

Church who go abroad to 'break new ground' are known to do two things; first they build a church, then they make a football pitch. In our organizations we certainly need both; but notice 'first they build a church'. Unless we put before our boys first the Church and all that it stands for, our work is surely of little permanent value. To say that they don't want religion is not only false, but clearly beside the point. Boys have ever been the same; and as our Lord when a boy was eager to know more about religion, and was found by His parents sitting in the midst of the doctors, asking them questions, so, too, the boy of today is equally interested. 'The religion of the inarticulate', as Donald Hankey called it, is not the religion of indifference; and because people are unwilling to speak about religion, it does not mean that they are not interested. Indeed, this book would seem to prove that that is far from being the case.

With these questions before me, it struck me that surely this would be a great and unique opportunity for some of our finest scholars and churchmen, men whose books and articles are usually impossible for a boy to understand, to help youth in a very real way. Could they not help our boys to understand better the great truths of our religion by giving them in as simple and short a way as possible the great benefit of their knowledge and experience? But . . . would they do it? Hopefully, I approached Professor A. E. Taylor and Professor H. R. Mackintosh; and, with the kindness and courtesy so characteristic of them, they readily agreed to help us. The first answers were printed in our club magazine, *The Canongate Chronicle*, and in that way our book began to grow.

To thank all the contributors for their interest and help seems but a small way of appreciating all that they have done for us. Great, indeed, has been the privilege of our boys to have had the opportunity of 'sitting among the doctors', and, as it were, 'asking them questions'. We felt that others should have a chance of sharing this privilege; for boys are very much the same everywhere; our boys' questions must be other boys' questions (and are not most *men*, in matters of religion, very much boys!). And so this book is published in the hope that it may help others, whether boys, or girls, or their leaders, as much as it has helped us.

Not all the papers are easy to understand; some require careful thought, and help from older people; but it is not a bad thing for a boy to find that truth is not always easily comprehensible: many things may be seen through a glass darkly:

> '. . . a man's reach should exceed his grasp,
> Or what's heaven for?'

Some difficult or uncommon words are explained in the index at the end.

RONALD SELBY WRIGHT

Contents

Note	5
From the Preface to the First Series.	8
What do you mean by 'Leading a Christian Life'?	15
W. R. INGE, sometime Dean of St. Paul's.	
In the Sense that No One really 'knows', are not all Men Agnostics?	21
JOHN BAILLIE, Principal and Professor of Theology, New College, Edinburgh University.	
Who Made God?	26
H. R. MACKINTOSH, sometime Professor of Systematic Theology, New College, Edinburgh University.	
Is God really Almighty?	29
A. E. Taylor, sometime Professor of Moral Philosophy, Edinburgh University.	
If God Made Everything, Who Made Evil?	38
C. C. MARTINDALE, S.J.	
Is there a Definite Evil Power that attacks People in the Same Way as there is a Good Power that influences People?	43
DOROTHY L. SAYERS.	
Why do You believe in God, and how can It help You?	53
G. F. FISHER, Archbishop of Canterbury.	
Why, if God is Love and Almighty, and if He loves every one individually, does He permit such happenings as Earthquakes, causing the awful death of thousands?	57
A. F. WINNINGTON INGRAM, sometime Bishop of London.	
If God guides Us, how do the Consciences of Christians differ so often, for example, in Politics?	61
W. R. MATTHEWS, Dean of St. Paul's.	
Does God really take any Notice of Our Prayers?	65
LINDSAY DEWAR, Principal of Bishop's College, Cheshunt.	

How can God be Watching over Every One and Listening to Every One's Prayers at Once? . . 69
  CHARLES E. RAVEN, sometime Regius Professor of Divinity, Cambridge University.

What was Christ's Position as God, if He prayed to God? 73
  L. W. GRENSTED, sometime Nolloth Professor of the Philosophy of the Christian Religion, Oxford University.

If Christ was God, How did God look after the World while Christ was in Palestine? . . . 77
  D. M. BAILLIE, Professor of Systematic Theology, St. Andrews University.

Can you Prove that Jesus Lived: Historically? . 83
  EDWYN BEVAN, sometime Honorary Fellow of New College, Oxford.

What are We to make of Jesus Christ? . . 87
  C. S. LEWIS, Fellow of Magdalen College, Oxford.

Do you need to Believe in the Virgin Birth to be a Christian? 93
  PAUL BULL, C.R.

Did not Some One have to betray Jesus, to fulfil the Scriptures; so why blame Judas, or for that matter, Pontius Pilate? If Christ had to be Crucified, in what way was His Crucifixion Wrong? . . . 101
  C. H. DODD, sometime Norris-Hulse Professor of Divinity, Cambridge University.

Why did Christ Work Miracles? Did He need to? . 107
  EDGAR P. DICKIE, Professor of Divinity, St. Andrews University.

Can you Prove that the Story of the Resurrection is True? 114
  GEORGE F. MACLEOD, Leader of the Iona Community.

What do You mean by the 'Fall' of Man? . . 119
  DAVID H. C. READ, Chaplain of Edinburgh University.

In What Way is Christ my Saviour? The Redemption .   123
M. C. D'ARCY, S.J.

What is 'The Holy Spirit'?   .   .   .   127
K. E. KIRK, Bishop of Oxford.

What is the Soul?   130
W. R. SORLEY, sometime Professor of Moral Philosophy,
Cambridge University.

Do you Believe in the Resurrection of the Body?   .   134
LORD QUICKSWOOD, sometime Provost of Eton College.

*Do we Really Know Anything at all about Life after
Death?*   139
PAT McCORMICK, sometime Vicar of St. Martin's in
the Fields, London.

*Is there no 'Eternal Life' for Good People who Lived
before Christ?*   145
NATHANIEL MICKLEM, Principal and Professor of Dog-
matic Theology, Mansfield College, Oxford.

Is there Such a Place as Hell?   .   .   .   150
L. S. THORNTON, C.R.

*Is it Possible to Reconcile the Thought of Eternal
Punishment with an All-Loving God?*   .   .   155
A. F. WINNINGTON-INGRAM, sometime Bishop of London.

*'Lead us not into Temptation'—but Would God Lead
us into Temptation?*   157
T. W. MANSON, Rylands Professor of Biblical Criticism
and Exegesis, Manchester University.

*Why does God make Sin so Easy and Goodness so
Difficult?*   162
Monsignor RONALD A. KNOX.

Why is it wrong to do Wrong?   .   .   .   169
R. W. MOORE, Head Master of Harrow.

What is Salvation?   174
D. S. CAIRNS, sometime Principal, Christ's College,
Aberdeen University.

How can We be the Men God wants Us to be? . 181
J. T. CHRISTIE, Principal of Jesus College, Oxford.

How is it Possible for us to be like Our Lord Jesus Christ? 187
C. C. J. WEBB, sometime Oriel Professor of the Philosophy of the Christian Religion, Oxford University.

Why do You believe in the Church and how can It help You? 194
G. F. FISHER, Archbishop of Canterbury.

Does a Christian need to go to Church? . . 198
W. D. MAXWELL, Minister of Whitekirk and Tyninghame, East Lothian.

Isn't Christianity 'played out'? . . . 204
JOHN MACMURRAY, Professor of Moral Philosophy, University of Edinburgh.

What are We to make of the Old Testament? . 212
GABRIEL HEBERT, S.S.M.

Where the Four Gospels don't Agree, Which One are We to Believe? 218
JAMES MOFFAT, sometime Washburn Professor of Church History, Union Theological Seminary, New York.

Can we Believe all the things we read of in the New Testament? 225
G. S. DUNCAN, Professor of Biblical Criticism and Principal of St. Mary's College, St. Andrews University.

Did not St. Paul spoil the Simple Religion of Jesus? . 232
J. S. STEWART, Professor of New Testament Language, Literature, and Theology, Edinburgh University.

What became of the Apostles? Why do we hear so little about them? 237
M. R. JAMES, sometime Provost of Eton College.

Shouldn't all Christians be Pacifists? . . 242
A. D. RITCHIE, Professor of Logic and Metaphysics, Edinburgh University.

SUBJECT-INDEX AND GLOSSARY . . 248

What do you mean by 'Leading a Christian Life'?

CHRISTIANITY is good news, not good advice. We Christians believe that Jesus Christ came into the world to assure us of certain facts about God our Father in heaven, and about ourselves as His children. Whether we believe all that the creeds tell us about the Person of Christ or not, it is certain that with Him a new faith and hope came into the world, which have had a greater and more enduring influence than can be attributed to any other man who has ever lived. The first Christians felt at once that the Gospel had changed everything for them. They spoke of 'a new creation'. 'Behold, I make all things new.' The New Testament is full of such phrases, confident and jubilant. In St. Paul's epistles we find a number of new words for moral qualities or aspects of the spiritual life—either words which were not in general use at all, or which were now used in a new sense. Such are the Greek words for love, humility, joy, hope, faith, and grace. People do not coin new words to express old ideas. If we want to know what Christianity was like when it was fresh from the mint, we can hardly do better than study these words in the places where they occur, and try to understand what they conveyed to St. Paul and his contemporaries.

Can we sum up in a few words what the message of the Gospel is? To begin with, God is our Father, and we are immortal spirits on our probation. So far as we know, our final destiny—either to live with other blessed spirits in the presence of God, or to be excluded from blessedness for ever—depends on how we spend the few years of our life on earth. Our Lord revealed to us a new standard of values, which demonetizes much of the

B

world's currency. Love is the primary virtue; those who
love God and their fellow men 'have fulfilled the law';
all the commandments are 'briefly comprehended in the
saying, Thou shalt love thy neighbour as thyself'. This
is rather different from the Jewish idea of 'righteousness'
—obedience to a just but 'jealous' God. It is different
from the Greek morality, which made 'justice' the chief
virtue. 'Render to all their dues' sums up the prevailing
Greek notion of our duty to God and to our neighbour,
and they coupled it with 'Nothing too much'.

We must not interpret Christian love as mere sentimentality. It includes genuine sympathy. 'Rejoice with
them that rejoice, and weep with them that weep.'
Seneca the Stoic says that only weak eyes weep over the
misfortunes of others; this is the great difference between
Christianity and Stoicism, which was in many ways a
noble creed. Almost all the philosophies offer to make
a man invulnerable; Christ did not. The Christian is
not afraid of suffering; he even welcomes it, and 'takes
up his cross' to follow his Master; but he does it from
'love of the brethren'.

But sympathy is not always easy. We are bidden to
love those whom we do not like. Is this possible? If we
sincerely wish them well, if we do them a good turn when
we can, and help them (if we have an opportunity) to
behave better or less badly than they seemed likely to
do, we have done what is possible, and we shall probably
discover that hardly any one is unlovable through and
through. We should make a point of remembering our
enemies in our prayers.

It was part of our Lord's standard of values that He
gave very small importance to the accessories and para-
phernalia of life. He belonged Himself to an independent, well-educated peasantry, who lived in very simple
comfort. He probably thought that this was the most
favourable condition of life. Money-grubbing He de-

spised, and thought that the anxieties which are insepar-
able from the possession of wealth are a very serious
hindrance to the higher life. No other moralist has
treated 'worry' so severely. But He was not an ascetic;
the hardships which He willingly endured were part of
His mission as a wandering preacher. He 'went into
society' when it came His way, attended social functions,
and accepted hospitality from the rich.

He pointedly refused to have anything to do with
economic disputes; they were not His business. The
covetous man is 'thou fool'; He never calls him a thief.

All moral improvement must come from within. From
within, out of the heart of man, comes all that can elevate
and all that can defile the character. Clean the inside of
the cup, not the outside. There is no political alchemy
which can get golden conduct out of leaden instincts.
A good tree cannot bring forth evil fruit, nor a corrupt
tree good fruit. This, as Thomas Carlyle said, is the
immense difference of the Gospel of Christ from the
gospel of Rousseau, who taught that the individual is
always good, and institutions always evil. 'If a vessel is
not clean', says Horace, speaking, this time, like a Christian, 'whatever you put into it turns sour.'

All man-made barriers our Lord levelled by ignoring
them. In Christ there is no difference between rich and
poor, Jew and Greek, civilized man and barbarian, free
man and slave.

Self-sacrifice is the only way to self-realization. He
who wishes to save his life (or his soul, as it is in the Greek)
shall lose it; and he who is willing to lose his life or soul
—his very self—for Christ's sake shall find it unto life
eternal.

The gospel of love needs no codes of morality, no lists
of virtues and sins, no legislation. Christ gives us hardly
any rules—only general principles, which we can apply
to our own problems, which may be sometimes rather

unlike those which came within His purview. This is why the ethics of the Gospel are never out of date.

What are the sins which He hated? For Christ did hate; His language of censure is very severe. I think we may say that He hated three things, which are often combined in the type of character which He abhorred. The first is hypocrisy, which means literally wearing a mask, like the ancient actors. The hypocrite need not be a Tartuffe or a Pecksniff; he is simply a man who hides his real character, motives, and ambitions. The Christian must be sincere and straightforward in thought, word, and deed. Next, our Lord hated hardness of heart, and all sins against charity. Thirdly, he hated calculating worldliness. As compared with other moralists, He was rather gentle to the merely disreputable faults, of which the doer himself is ashamed, and stern against those which proceed from low aims and deliberate selfishness, the sins of a strong character.

This teaching was grievously distorted in the post-apostolic Church. Lists of virtues and sins were drawn up, with a mechanical system of penances. The two worst offences, ranking with murder, were adultery and apostasy, the latter including any defection from the one privileged institutional Church. Virginity became the almost indispensable rule for those who aspired to 'perfection . Asceticism in its extremist forms was highly honoured. Cruelty has no place among the deadly sins. Later, when the northern nations established themselves in the Mediterranean lands, some new features were introduced into the accepted ideal—chivalry, with the northern code of honour, and romanticism, a strange blend of nobility and folly.

With the Reformation came the characteristic 'intra-mundane asceticism' of Calvin, emphasizing the duty of work, and the happiness which follows profitable industry and strict self-control. For the first time, Christianity reconciled itself with industrialism, and tried to hallow the life of the man of business.

The lay standard of morality at the present time may be described as humanism, the ingredients of which are —traditional Christian ethics; the northern code of honour, which we prefer to call being 'decent' and avoiding things which are 'not done'; a vague utilitarian or hedonistic standard—'try to give every one a good time'; and a very genuine detestation of cruelty, ingratitude, and treachery. It falls short of the Christian standard in not recognizing the 'offence of the cross'—the stern truth that gain comes through pain, victory through defeat; in the vagueness of its values; in the secularity of its aims, forgetting that our earthly life is a pilgrimage to the heavenly city; and, in a word, in its want of heroism. Its lack of discipline prevents it from being the adequate morality of a strong and healthy society.

Are there any duties which we now ought to recognize, though they are not emphasized in the New Testament? The early Christians had no wish to take part in politics, but there were no politics for them to take part in while they lived under a despotism. The Christian citizen of a free country is in a different position. He ought to take his part in public affairs. But, as Plato and St. Paul agree, our real citizenship is in heaven, and if we mix in secular politics, our marching orders must be, 'See that thou make all things according to the pattern shown thee in the mount.'

Science has enormously lengthened our expectation of life, as a species, on this earth. From this follow certain duties not recognized in antiquity—thought for the welfare of posterity, which may include eugenics; the duty of not wasting or defacing the natural resources and beauties of our home; and, we may add, our duties to the lower animals, who, as we now recognize, have rights which should be respected.

I think I have made it sufficiently clear what 'leading a Christian life' means. I need only add that it is a definite call to come out of the ruck, to go into hard training, and to choose a mode of life which will involve much self-denial and great strength of will. Our Lord made it very clear that His Gospel will never be popular: 'Strait is the gate and narrow is the way that leadeth unto life, and few there be that find it.'

W. R. INGE

In the Sense that No One really 'knows', are not All Men Agnostics?

OF the deep mystery that surrounds our human situation there can indeed be no doubt. Such understanding as we have of it shades off at all points into ignorance. It is not thinkable that available knowledge will ever keep pace with our human inquisitiveness, or that the best-instructed parents will ever be able to answer all the questions put to them even by their six-year-old children. The farther we press back our speculations, the more hazardous do our conclusions become, and it is only the most superficial and least imaginative thinkers whose degree of assurance has not diminished as they continued their probings to ever more remote regions of inquiry. The great thinkers, the real *brooders*, have always been keenly aware of the narrow limits within which certain knowledge was possible to them, and have not exaggerated the measure of probability attaching to each successive step in their speculative progress. Or, when the academic philosophers have failed us in this respect, the poets have usually been at hand to help. It is on the sense of mystery that poetry feeds. Where all the outlines are clear and hard there is opportunity neither for poetic feeling nor for poetic vision. But we cannot read the Book of Job or the Book of Psalms, Aeschylus or Sophocles, Shakespeare or Goethe, without being made deeply aware of the solemnity of our human situation, the pathos of our ignorance, the poignancy of our unsatisfied desire. If agnosticism meant only the recognition of the vast area of uncertainty that surrounds the little knowledge we possess, then indeed all truly reflective spirits must be agnostic.

However, what agnosticism usually means is not that, but rather the denial that we have any reliable knowledge at all about the ultimate meaning and background of our human situation. The first thing to be said about such a denial is that it would kill poetic feeling and vision just as effectively as would the completest dogmatism. Poetry can as little live where all is mysterious as where nothing is, as little where all is darkness as where all is light.

Fortunately, however, pure agnosticism is an exceedingly rare phenomenon, if not indeed a non-existent one. Probably the nearest approach to it is in the thought of T. H. Huxley, who invented the term. There have, of course, been many others who sincerely believed themselves to be agnostics; but they have never been consistent in their profession of ignorance, never really quite neutral in their attitude towards the different varieties of possible belief. In practically every case they have been men who rejected such knowledge as was offered to them by the religious tradition in which they were reared, or by which they were surrounded, and who professed to have nothing at all of a positive kind to put in its place. But actually they always had something; and very often they were no less dogmatic about this alternative than were their opponents about the traditional view.

The professed agnosticism of modern times has appeared for the most part within the frontiers of Christendom, and the knowledge it has been concerned to repudiate has been the knowledge offered in the Christian revelation (but including also the conclusions reached by the idealist philosophers). To be fully consistent, its contention should have been that the Christian view of things is quite as likely to be true as any other, but no more likely—we just do not know. This is the position Huxley tried to maintain, but it is very doubtful whether he succeeded in doing so. He wrote: 'If there is anything in the world that I do firmly believe in, it is the universal validity of the law of causation, but that universality cannot be proved by any amount of experience.' Here he was already accepting something that went beyond the evidence of the senses, and on the basis of it he developed a definite view of the background of our human situation, namely, that we are enmeshed in a cosmic process which is definitely anti-moral in its tendency.

Next to Huxley, the name of agnostic is most prominently associated with his contemporary, Herbert Spencer, who gave the name of 'The Unknowable' to the ultimate reality behind the world of sense. But Spencer gave such an account of the *knowable* (in terms of the indestructibility of matter and energy, and of an evolutionary rhythm governing mental and moral as well as physical processes) as to lend a definitely materialist colouring to his Unknowable. Of other agnostics it may be said with confidence that in the end they will be found putting forward some alternative view of the nature of things which, to say the very least, they believe to be *more* probable than the Christian one. It is really impossible for the human spirit to rest in a state of complete neutrality concerning the meaning and purpose of human existence, or (what is the same thing) concerning its relation to the background of ultimate reality against which it is set. We obviously cannot live and act without adopting some kind of positive attitude towards at least the foreground of existence—the use we make of our own lives, our relation to our fellows, and the goals of our common striving; but in so doing we are inevitably basing ourselves upon certain presuppositions, whether consciously realized or otherwise, concerning the background of our existence. In this sense it is true that nobody is really an agnostic.

Let us now consider what the Christian religion has to say on the matter. The sense of the mystery of existence is nowhere more strongly felt and expressed than it is in the Bible. The smallness of our knowledge in comparison with the vast extent of our ignorance is everywhere recognized. The mind and purposes of God are said to be largely inscrutable. 'Canst thou by searching find out God?' 'When he hideth his face, who can behold him?' 'Clouds and darkness are round about him.' 'How unsearchable are his judgements, and his ways past finding out! For who hath known the mind of the Lord? or who hath been his counsellor?' 'As the heavens are higher than the earth, so are my ways higher than your ways, and my thoughts than your thoughts.'

But what the Christian Gospel claims to do is to pierce this darkness and mystery with a bright ray of light. This is typified in the story of the Magi: 'And lo, the star which they saw in the east, went before them, till it came and stood over where the young child was. When they saw the star, they rejoiced with exceeding great joy.' The Magi were men who had long been seeking a clue to the ultimate mystery, and the story says that at last they found it in the Babe of Bethlehem. That is where Christians find their clue. They believe that all we need to know about the meaning and purpose of existence is revealed to us in Jesus Christ. 'In him was life; and the life was the light of men. And the light shineth in the darkness. . . . That was the true Light, which lighteth every man that cometh into the world. . . . No man hath seen God at any time; the only begotten Son, which is in the bosom of the Father, he hath declared him' [or 'made him known'].

Even when the revelation of God in Jesus Christ is thus accepted and believed, the mystery remains. Our natural human inquisitiveness still remains largely unsatisfied. We continue to ask all sorts of questions to which we can find no answer. The light that has been vouchsafed to us is not nearly all we could desire. But is it not all we really need? Can we justly, in view of what God has given us in Jesus Christ, complain that we have not now enough light to live by—and to see to do our work by? Such a complaint would seem to be unreasonable, until we are able to say that we have already availed ourselves fully of such light as has been given us. And which of us can say that? However much there may be that is still hidden from us, we all know enough to be much better than we are. Let us then stop airing our agnosticisms until we have done something about this prior situation—until we have faced up to the challenge of Christ. For no further light is likely to break in upon us until we have made better use of the light we already have.

JOHN BAILLIE

Who Made God?

THIS is a question often asked, and I suppose a question which many people have found it very difficult to answer. Let us see for a moment what can be done with it.

To begin with, it might not be a bad thing to inquire whether the question 'Who made God?' has any real meaning at all. Because, of course, if it has no *meaning* whatever, to answer it will not be easy. And remember there are plenty of questions which don't have any meaning. You can manufacture dozens of them if you try. You might even play a game of making them up. Here are two: How much does the Calton Hill love Leith Walk? Or again: Why is a top when it spins? Years ago we used to ask each other that second puzzle as a good joke; but it had no more meaning than the answer, which was: Because the higher the fewer. So that some questions can be quite meaningless. Perhaps the question 'Who made God?' is one of them.

If only we consider what the word *God* stands for, it rather looks as if this were the case here. What ought to be in our minds when we utter that great Name? The Apostles' Creed is a fairly good guide. There we find God described as 'the Father Almighty, Maker of heaven and earth'. That tells us that He made everything there is. But if He made everything there is, it is not easy to see how anything could be left over which could make *Him*. Whatever might be named as having created God would, of course, turn out to have been created by Him first, for after all it would be one of the things 'in heaven and earth'.

Let me emphasize three points, or rather let me state one point in three different ways.

1. If you say 'Who made God?' you imply that some-

body or something existed before God, with the power to call Him into being. Let us call this somebody or something XY. Now we seem to have got everything nicely settled: we know now who made God. It was XY. But at once, if you tell this to a friend, he replies: But who made XY, please? And if you have your answer ready and say—Who made XY? Why, of course it was AB. Then instantly he asks: And who made AB? And so it goes on for ever. You just go round and round in a circle, aimlessly. All your questions and answers leave you exactly where you were at the start.

2. If you say 'Who made God?' that implies that we can really form the idea of a 'made' God. But *made* and *God* are words—the one an adjective, the other a noun— that simply won't go together. They are like oil and water; they won't mix. Not all adjectives suit all nouns. I can speak of a piercing sound, but I can't speak of a green sound. If I talk about a sweet taste, people understand me perfectly, but not if I talk of a square taste. A square taste is nothing at all. And in the same way, a 'made' God is nothing at all. The adjective and the noun fly apart as soon as you try to connect them with each other. Wood made of iron is not really wood, and a made God is not really God.

3. If you say 'Who made God?' what you have in mind is not the idea of God, but the idea of an idol. Among heathen nations to-day, just as in Bible times, the village carpenter makes an idol or little god out of wood, and he uses the chips left over when the idol has been made to cook his dinner. You will find all that described, with scorn and irony, in the 44th chapter of Isaiah. But then an idol is not God. An idol is something that men kick downstairs when it has disappointed them. But God is He who created us and in Christ has redeemed us.

Perhaps you may ask, But why should we just have to accept the fact that you can't go behind God and tell how

He came to be made? Well, in science as much as in religion we have simply to accept things. Scientific men to-day assure us that there can be no movement in the universe more rapid than the movement of light. The speed of light is 186,000 miles per second. Why should that be the swiftest motion that is possible in the world? Nobody knows why, but it is.

What would Jesus Christ have said if we had gone up to Him and said: 'Who made God?' I think He would have smiled—a friendly smile, of course. But if you had spent a day in His company, after an hour or two you would have felt that the notion of a 'made' God could not have entered His mind. When He said: 'I thank Thee, O Father, Lord of heaven and earth', He was thinking of 'the everlasting God, the Lord, the Creator of the ends of the earth'. God is before all things, and for His pleasure they are and were created.

HUGH R. MACKINTOSH

Is God really Almighty?

'THE Lord God *omnipotent* reigneth.' What does this mean? Perhaps it is more profitable to ask what the text does *not* mean. To begin with, we should note that the word, in our English Bible, is a rendering of the Greek *pantocratōr*, itself a translation employed in the Greek version of the Old Testament of epithets applied to God in the Hebrew Scriptures. The original sense of these epithets is of course a matter for Hebrew scholars, and it may well be that, in the case of some of them, it is no longer certainly discoverable. But we have a much larger stock of Greek than of Hebrew literature, and this should enable us to say at least what the word *pantocratōr* presumably meant to the Greek translators of the Old Testament, and therefore to the New Testament writers whose minds were saturated with ideas derived from the Greek translation of the Old.

Consider the great outstanding difference between the conception of God preached by the great Hebrew prophets and that commonly current—except for a few philosophers—in the contemporary Gentile world. The Gentiles at large were 'polytheistic'. They believed in 'gods many and lords many'. Each of these gods might be the supreme power in a certain district, or in a certain department of affairs, but there are other districts and other departments, and these too have their own gods. The Hebrews themselves had thought no differently in the pre-prophetic days. The Lord, as Jephthah puts it, has given Canaan to the children of Israel but equally Chemosh has given their own territory to his people, the children of Ammon. When David takes refuge with the King of Gath he assumes as a matter of course that for the present he must 'serve other gods', those of the land in which he now finds himself.

The common view of the Graeco-Roman world was rather different. They tended to hold that it is the same gods who exert their power in all lands alike, though in different places they are known by different names and worshipped with different rites. But each of these gods has his own particular department of nature, and it is only within that department that he is supreme. Neptune, for example, is all-powerful on the seas, but it is not his concern what happens on the dry land. Mars is the god of battles, but it is not Mars whom you trust in times of peace to watch over flocks and herds, or the fruits of the earth; these have their own divine protectors. In a Pantheon of this kind there is really no power which is supreme over all the affairs of a man's life, none can be a 'present help' in every time of trouble, or can be looked to 'to supply *all* our need'. And it is only too probable that one such departmental deity will be at complete cross-purposes with another. If one is like Baal-zebub of Ekron, interested in flies, and another in fruits, the two are not very likely to see eye to eye. A 'nature-polytheism' of numerous departmental 'gods' thus leaves little or no room for any real belief in the supreme direction of human life or the course of nature by any single wise and benevolent divine purpose. Where there are many 'gods' there is in reality *no God*. It is not surprising that the working 'religion' of the Roman Empire in the days of our Lord seems to have been a belief in blind Fortune or Luck as the real ruler of the world. By the time of our Lord and St. Paul this deification of an irrational and immoral Luck had taken a particularly deadly form in consequence of the *astrological* superstition which, though completely unknown to the Greeks of the best ages, had been introduced from the East after the conquests of Alexander the Great. The caprices of Fortune were supposed to be registered in advance in the heavens, particularly in the movements of the planets, and the planets were very widely supposed to be agents who are not merely non-moral or unbenevolent but positively malignant to man. It is they who are apparently meant in the Epistle to the Ephesians by the 'world-rulers [the *cosmocratores*, the word is an astrological technicality] of this darkness' against which the Christian's life is an unbroken combat. A man was thought of as, in every act, a mere helpless slave of the 'stars' which 'ruled' at the moment of his birth or his conception, doomed once for all to be rich or poor, high or low, happy or miserable, wise or foolish, good or bad, by the configuration of the heavens revealed by his horoscope, and without any power of helping himself, a mere puppet of forces of which all we can say is that their working discloses no supreme coherent purpose and, so far as we can guess at any purpose underlying it, they appear to be actually malevolent. The moral attitude towards the problems of life inspired by such a superstition must at best be a listless indifferentism, at worst an audacious and unscrupulous recklessness, or a hopeless despair, according as you believe yourself to have been born under a lucky or unlucky conjunction of stars and planets.

The New Testament conception of God as *pantocratōr* is, in the first instance, a message of practical hope and comfort for those oppressed by these polytheistic and astrological superstitions, men who have only in adult life escaped from them and are in constant danger of relapsing into them. We shall see its full meaning best if we render the word not by *omnipotent*, but more literally by *supreme over everything*, or *supreme everywhere*. According to the current polytheistic ideas, a god may be, let us say, 'Lord of Rhodes' but powerless in Africa, he may rule the waves at his will but his dominion ceases at the shore, he may be the 'God of Battles', but

C

there are other gods of the arts of peace, and they may
be at enmity with him, so that you can only secure their
help by doing what will make him your foe. Christianity, like Judaism, proclaims that its God is supreme
in Rhodes and Africa, on sea and land, in war and
peace equally and alike, and that He is good in all his
ways. There is therefore a single wise and good purpose
throughout the course of *all* that happens, and that a
purpose which cannot be thwarted. There is no other
deity whose ill will you incur by your obedience to the
will of *our* God, and no contingency in life where He
cannot support and sustain you against all opposition.
And the prevalent astrological superstition and the
despair and sense of human impotence that it breeds are
alike vain. We need not suppose that St. Paul held our
modern view of astrology as an empty delusion. His
language suggests rather that, like most men of his age,
he believed in the reality of malign 'planetary in-
fluences', as he probably believed many other things
that we now know not to be true. His point is that
however evil and however powerful the 'world-rulers'
may be, they can be resisted and defeated, for there is a
power which is greater than theirs, they are the *cosmocratores*, but it is God, and not they, who is *pantocratōr*,
supreme over all. To use the language of the astrologers
themselves, there is a ruler of the 'house of life', but that
ruler is not Jupiter nor Lucifer, son of the morning, it is
'the Father of our Lord Jesus Christ', and with Him for
us, it matters little that all the 'stars in their courses'
should be against us. The New Testament doctrine of
the omnipotence of God is thus tantamount to the
simple statement that the whole course of the history
of the world and of man is controlled by a single all-
wise and all-good will, and that this will is supreme;
there is no power in heaven or in earth that can thwart
it or deflect it from the achievement of its purpose. And

consequently our own will, too, is secured against defeat just in so far as it can be made one with God's.

There is no sign that the Christians of the apostolic days perplexed themselves with the curious and sometimes impertinent speculative questions about the extent of the divine omnipotence which were mooted in later ages by the acute metaphysicians of the schools. Much of this speculation may not unreasonably strike us as neither very profitable nor very reverent. Yet there is one valuable lesson we may learn from it. John Stuart Mill was quite mistaken about his facts when he complained that though the theologians had discovered all sorts of qualifications and limitations upon the *goodness* of God, they had never considered any possible limitations to God's power. As Mansel was prompt to remind him, the schoolmen had actually made long lists of 'things which God cannot do'. Omnipotence never meant to them what might be expressed in our modern slang as the ability to do 'any old thing'. It was laid down that not God Himself can do what is in its own nature absurd and contradictory. Thus it was said that God cannot create another God, i.e. another creator of all things, since a created Creator is a contradiction in terms. Again, God cannot undo the past in the sense of making it untrue that an event which has happened has happened (God, it was held, can no doubt bring a dead man back to life, but God Himself, though He may raise Lazarus, cannot make it true that Lazarus did not die, if Lazarus in fact has died). This inability to do what is in its own nature impossible and absurd is no real limitation of the divine power. So again it is no real defect of power in God that, being as He is absolutely and perfectly good, God *cannot* will to sin, any more than it is lack of knowledge in Him that He cannot think that to be true which is untrue. The defect, or limitation, is in beings like ourselves, who can will to do what is wrong or can believe what is false.

All this may sound academic and perhaps a little trivial, but it leads up to a further consideration which we too often forget, with the consequence that we create unnecessary difficulties for ourselves about divine omnipotence.

We must add, I think, that not only cannot even an almighty will will to do what is in its own nature self-contradictory: further, a perfectly wise and perfectly good God cannot be false to His own purposes, and therefore He cannot will to do anything that, without being *self-contradictory*, conflicts with His own supreme purpose in the government of His creatures. If it is His purpose in creating us to call into being free and intelligent agents who may be not His puppets but His fellow workers willingly co-operating with His plans for themselves, and to *educate* them into such co-operation, then, in order that we may learn to choose to co-operate with Him, we must also be able, if we please, to refuse to co-operate; we must be free to choose wrongly as well as to choose rightly. It follows that God himself cannot, without stultifying His own purpose with us, simply force us to will right 'whether or not'. It is *perhaps* in itself conceivable that mankind might have been so created that they needed no such education, endowed with an intelligence which could invariably discern the path of right and a devotion to it which no temptation could assail. But what is certain is that this is not the plan which our Creator has followed with us. For His own good reasons He has chosen the other course, and since He has done so, it is no real restriction of His omnipotence that in His dealings with us He does not stultify His own plan by miraculously intervening to frustrate all the consequences of men's thoughtlessness or their deliberate choice of evil. To be false to His own purpose would no more be 'power' in God than it is in man.

It is true that when kindly hearted men contemplate the evil and misery of a world-war, when they consider the degradation in which its instigators plunge themselves, the untold suffering in which they involve millions of their fellow men, and the inevitable lowering of the moral standards brought about even in those who take arms to defend the 'elemental decencies', they find themselves impelled to ask despairingly how an almighty God can 'let such things happen'. But if we will reflect, we can see, I think, that the question itself implies an assumption which we should find unworthy of us. It is assumed that the purpose of a wise and good Creator can only be to give His creatures as much pleasure and as little pain as possible, regardless of the sources from which the pleasure and the pain are derived, to make them all 'happy' at the least cost. And certainly the occurrence of wars would be sufficient proof that if this is really our Creator's purpose, He must be unable to carry it out; there must be powers at work in the universe which are refractory to His design and too formidable for Him to cope with. But let us ask ourselves seriously whether we can think such a purpose as this worthy of the All-wise and All-good. Must we not agree with Kant that a Creator whose one purpose was simply to give us pleasure and to spare us pain would not be a Creator whom we could *reverence*, and that it would be thinking more worthily of God to say that His purpose with us is not simply to 'make us happy', but to make us the kind of persons who *deserve* to be happy? Or, if you like to put the thought rather differently, to teach us by the discipline of life to find happiness in the right things? (And the 'right thing', as Kant himself insists, in spite of his anxiety to avoid the language of devotional 'unction', is a will conformed throughout to the 'holy' will of God.) Happiness, as we all know, is a word which means the most different things to different men. To many of us at all times, as I suppose to all of us at some times, it means much that is frivolous and foolish and merely sensual; there are those to whom it means the gratification of unbridled ambition or lust of power. In fact, to 'make a man happy' means the same thing as to give him all he wants, and the trouble is that all of us for some of the time, and many of us for all of the time, want the things which are not worth having. It takes time and discipline, and often very costly discipline, to learn to set our hearts on the things which are really worth having; the serious business of our lives is not to get all we happen to want so much as to learn to want what we ought to want. So long as that lesson is not duly learned, it is inevitable that our wanting the wrong things should make havoc of our own life and the lives of others who are so closely bound up with us in the solidarity of our kind. Why the lesson should be as costly as it is, why we cannot learn sufficiently to set our hearts on the right things at less expenditure of blood and tears to all mankind, is more than we can know fully. But if it is the main purpose of our Creator to teach His creatures the lesson, the costliness of the price is no sufficient reason for denying His omnipotence. It would only become so if we *knew* that, when the price has been paid, the lesson will not have been learned.

Let me end these poor remarks by quoting two typical and quite unmetaphysical expressions of the substance of the Christian's faith in the omnipotence of his God. The first is the familiar passage of St. Paul: 'Who shall separate us from the love of Christ? Shall tribulation, or distress, or persecution, or famine, or nakedness, or peril, or sword? . . . Nay, in all these things we are more than conquerors through Him that loved us.' (It is not denied that 'these things' have to be faced and that they are grievous, but the point is that they can be faced and faced triumphantly 'through Him that loved us'.) The other, a less-known but worthy parallel, is from John Bunyan. (I regret that I have not at hand the volume of his minor works from which it is taken, and so cannot supply the precise reference.) 'Christ Jesus has bags of no one knows what laid up for no one knows who.'

A. E. TAYLOR

If God Made Everything, Who Made Evil?

THE question is an important one, so you will not expect the answer to be a cheap one, that you could rattle off in a line or two. We do not mean to shirk trying to give the answer as well as we can; and we can trust you to think it over as seriously as you can.

Evil is not a 'thing' at all. So no one could make it and no one ever did. 'But then', you say, 'if there isn't any evil, how can I call anything "bad"? Cannot I do any "bad" actions?'

What do I mean by 'bad'? I call a thing 'bad' when it has *not* got certain qualities that I judge it ought to have, in the circumstances. By a 'good' apple, I mean an apple that I can eat and enjoy. A 'bad' apple is either one that is not 'ripe'—that has *not* yet become juicy, or sweet enough: or, an apple that has become 'over-ripe'—that has *no more* got its firmness, or proper colour, or sweetness. But, N.B., all the chemicals that compose it—oxygen, hydrogen, &c.—are *perfectly good* chemicals, all the time. Suppose I give you a pencil and piece of paper, and say: 'Draw a circle.' You do so; and I say: 'That is a bad circle.' I do not mean that the line you have drawn is not a good line so far as that goes, but, it has *not* got the qualities that make it into a circle: it may be all sorts of other curves; but it is not 'circular'.

But now you might say, 'Well, but there are all sorts of qualities I haven't got, and things I can't do—I can't fly like a bird or jump like an antelope or stop under water like a fish. But you wouldn't call me a bad man for that?' Certainly not. I didn't say you called things 'bad' because they lacked just *any* sort of qualities, but because they lacked certain qualities they 'ought' to have—for instance, I don't say you have bad sight because you haven't got eight eyes—as a human creature you are not meant to have eight eyes: but I could say you had 'bad' sight if your two human eyes lacked something that they ought to have, if they are to be properly useful. For instance, if they are shaped so that you can't see at a reasonable distance—if they have *not* got the proper shape for doing so, *then* I can say you have 'bad' eyes.

So 'badness' is not a thing at all: it is the *absence* of something that 'ought' in the circumstances to be there. So God did not create 'badness': no one can create, or make, a 'non-thing'. This is by far the hardest part of our argument; but if you can see it, you will see all the rest.

Now what you are really worrying about is, not the 'badness' of an apple or an eye, but 'moral' badness; that is, badness in human men and women, which is really in their minds, though it may show itself in their decisions and their acts. But the same principle holds good. Suppose I take a knife and kill a man by stabbing him with it. Now my knife is good, all the muscular actions of my arm are good, my aim is good; but then I have *not* got a proper state of mind and will with regard to that man. Either I shut away from my mind all sorts of thoughts about him and myself—such as, that to kill him is cruel because he has a wife and children depending on him; or, that it is out of all proportion to kill a man because he has come across me while I was burgling his house; or, above all, that I, a mere man, simply have no right over the life of my fellow man—well, I may either *put* all this out of my mind; or fury may as it were 'black it out'—but in any case, certain thoughts are *not* in my mind which *ought* to be there.

Take a very important topic, which deserves to be spoken of very clearly and at greater length—a 'bad' use of your bodies. Now your bodies are part of God's creation and are good, and all their instincts are good. But I can misuse my body or instincts by shutting out certain thoughts from my mind. For instance, I can use my body properly, so as to become a father when I am married, and so make the most beautiful thing in the world—a good home and a happy family. But then, I can shut out all ideas about this full and proper use of myself, or again, 'blind' passion may possess me so that I don't think at all, or finally, I may feel that I 'can't' help myself. Then I shall make a 'wrong use' of my body, or allow my instincts to 'master' me. The result is, that I can do things that 'fall short' of the right action in the right circumstances *by so much*, that my action must be called 'wrong'.

All these and other 'wrong' actions come back in the long run to a form of selfishness. I *shut out* all the thoughts that I ought to have, as a man living 'socially' among men; and you see this especially on a large scale, as when there is a war, or a great fraud. Why do men commit fraud? Because they want to get something (money, or power) for *themselves*, without paying any attention to the people they get it from. Hence you may find a man, or a company, 'exploiting' his employees. (Do not forget that an employee can 'cheat' the man he has made an agreement with just as badly as the employer can cheat *him*.) Or you may find a country (which means its politicians) saying: 'I need a bit of territory and the trade it will bring in. Yes; I know it belongs to Africans: but they are mere niggers and they can't hurt me. Besides, France wants it, and so does Germany; and I must get it first, and if they try any games, I will go to war with them, I don't care how many lives it costs on this side or that!' Land lust; money lust—that is the origin of wars—it isn't God who makes them. It is myself, making a bad use, that is, a selfish use, of my intelligence and my power of choosing and deciding. I shut out any amount of things I ought to think of and remember, and concentrate on nothing but my personal or national advantages.

But finally, you might say: 'God *is* responsible, after

all, in the long run, because He made men *able* to *leave out* better and larger thoughts, and think only in a selfish way; and *able* to decide to act for the pleasure or advantage of the moment. Why did He not make them *unable* to think and choose anything save what was fully true and fully good?' The answer is: 'Because in that case they wouldn't have been *free* at all. It is better to be free— free even to do wrong—than to be *forced* even into doing good. If I couldn't help doing what was good, I should be like a machine, which can't help acting properly so long as it is properly stoked up and till its parts wear out. It is better to be a man than a machine.' You see? God would contradict Himself if He said: 'I give you Free Will', and then immediately *forced* your will into a 'one way' decision only.

So even moral evil comes about, you see, on a large or a small scale, from men shutting out a certain amount of truth from their minds, and then acting as though what they are not looking at does not exist. God creates man, and gives him certain powers, and then, man does *not* use those powers properly. It is always *man* who starts to do the act, which, in its circumstances, can be wrong; it is never God who forces him to, or creates a 'wrong' thing. And we really all know that. You cannot anywhere find a man or a race which does not see a difference between 'right' and 'wrong'. Men do not always put the difference in the same place; but even a native in the heart of Africa has a whole list of things he regards as 'wrong'. For instance, he may think it a true kindness to kill his parents once they get old and sick; but he would think it wrong to kill them while they were young and healthy. This is an affair of 'educating the conscience'. Besides, it is far more difficult for us to think clearly and choose properly than it should be, simply because men have done wrong for such a long time, and so many men do wrong round about us. There is a sort of 'current' of wrong ideas (such as that money is the only thing that counts, no matter how you get it), and of wrong behaviour (such as wrongdoing with women), that the man who wants to act right has to beat his way up-stream, so to say—against the current. But then, though God will not force you to do right—for He respects your free will—He will give you plenty of help. 'For them who love Him, God *makes* all things work together for good'—that is the right translation of St. Paul's words. 'But say what you will—it's very difficult!' Yes. But then you wouldn't insist, would you, on having a soft job merely? Christ is your friend, and your captain. You would feel rather second-rate if you said to Him: 'Oh yes, I'll do a job—but mind You make it soft!'

C. C. MARTINDALE, S. J.

Is there a Definite Evil Power that attacks People in the Same Way as there is a Good Power that influences People?

IT will perhaps be easier to answer this question if we ask first what the 'good power' is, and what it is like. If we are Christians, we do not talk about 'a good power', as though it were a mechanical force, like gravitation or electricity. We name it 'God', and speak of it as 'He'—that is to say, we believe it to be, not merely personal, but *a person*, with a single consciousness and a single will. We say also that God is the Creator— He *makes* things. He made the universe in which we live, and perhaps other universes of which we know nothing, imagining them into existence, we may say, out of His own mind, as a writer makes a book. And He is continually at work in His creation, keeping it in existence, renewing it, developing it, building it up. If His power were withdrawn from it for a moment, no two atoms could hold together—it would fall apart and vanish like a dream into the utter nothingness out of which He imagined it. It would simply cease to be, because 'to be' or 'to exist' means 'to be present in the mind of God'; He is all the real existence that there is, and apart from Him there is no other way of existing. And like every other person who makes a thing for his own pleasure, God loves what He makes, though, of course, to an infinitely greater degree than any human 'maker'. He does not get tired of it, or lose heart and patience, as we do; and when anything goes wrong with His creation, He does not throw it away in a fit of anger, but sets Himself to redeem the wrong, at whatever cost to Himself. The story of the Gospel is, in fact, the story of the personal sacrifice of God, entering His world to put right the wrong which we call 'sin'.

God is thus known and believed by Christians to be a united personality, a maker, a lover, and the one source of all real existence. If we ask, 'is God good?' we are really putting the question the wrong way round. 'Good' is the word we use to describe everything that is 'of God', which behaves in the way He intended it to behave, and which is like Him in being united, creative, loving, and *real*, because apart from God nothing can have any real existence.

That being so, how could anything evil get into the universe? How could the creation, or any part of it, 'go wrong'? That is the great and puzzling question. For the *fact* that something is very wrong with this planet on which we live is only too obvious. Man in particular is very far from being altogether united and loving, and much that he is and does is destructive rather than creative, and false rather than real or true.

God might, no doubt, have made a universe that 'went right' automatically, without any possibility of disobeying His will for it. Indeed, so far as we can tell, He did make a great many things of this kind. All the inorganic part of the universe appears to behave in an orderly and harmonious way. Rain falls, the sun shines, metals and crystals form themselves in the earth without question or complaint, and without rebellion. If lightning splits a rock, or the sea washes it away, the rock does not seem to mind—it has, apparently, no feelings to be hurt. Again, among the lower kind of living things, though ivy may smother a tree or weeds choke other flowers, change and dissolution seem to be accepted without resentment. Such creatures as these do what they have to do, and do nothing otherwise; indeed, they cannot do otherwise: they have no choice. But some other of His creatures were made by God with the power of choice; and Man is one of these. Man was made with a free will, so that his obedience to God's will might be, not an automatic necessity, but a spontaneous act. He was so made that he might do the harmonious, creative, loving, real and *good* thing—not because he was unable to do otherwise, but because he *wanted* to do it, and this was to be his happiness. When the Bible says that Man was made 'in the image of God', this is what it means: that he was to be a real person, like God, with a will to create and love, as God does, knowing what he was doing and desiring with all his nature to do it. And he was given a mind to understand that in so doing he was carrying out the will of God his maker, in whom his whole existence found its reality.

If you ask, 'Why did God make a creature of this kind?' it is difficult to answer, except by saying: 'Look into yourself, you who were made in God's image, and find the answer there.' It is good and pleasurable to make or possess a machine that goes well simply because it is made that way and cannot do otherwise. It does your will, and so far that is good. But it is a different kind of pleasure to have a son, or even a pet dog, that does things to please you because he understands what you want and eagerly desires to co-operate with you of his own accord, because he loves you and freely puts his will at your disposal. Your delight lies in his power of choice—in the fact that he *might* have chosen to oppose you, but instead *chose* to please you; he is not incapable of opposition, nor coerced into obedience by the arbitrary exercise of your power: he is free, and he is yours, and that is happiness for both of you.

But the fact that man has a *choice* offered to him brings us up against two very important facts about the whole creation, including mankind. The created universe is not only a made thing, dependent for its very existence upon the will and love of its Maker. It is, by its nature, *limited*. Choice, in fact, implies limitation— it means that you can be, or have, or do, these things *or* those things: you cannot be, have, and do everything. It also implies that there must be *differences* between one person and another, between one thing and another. If everybody and everything were merged in one great sameness, there would be no individual persons to choose, and no choice to be made.

There is nothing in itself evil about being limited and nothing in itself evil about there being differences. The difference of things is, in fact, (or should be) a source of perpetual delight to us. The amazing and intricate variety of people and things, the great number of possibilities open to us, are precisely what make the world so interesting and exciting. And this variety is (or should be) pleasant to us just *because* of our own limitations: we can take pleasure in the beauty of a tree, the charm of another person, because they are something other than ourselves. We are limited by nature: it is not in our power to *be* the tree or the other person; but that is the very reason why we are able to admire and love them. To each creature we can give the proper love and reverence which is due to it as something other than ourselves: to God, who is so infinitely other than ourselves, we can give the infinite love and reverence due to Him; and so live in harmony with God, and ourselves and the rest of the creation.

I say, 'we can'; but in fact we do not, and feel, indeed, that we cannot. We look at other people and, very often, hate them; we look at the world about us and, instead of loving and reverencing the things in it, we try to tyrannize over them, misuse them, snatch them away from other people, or smash and destroy them; we look at God and deliberately set our wills to thwart and disobey Him; and when we have done these things, we look at ourselves and snarl before the rage and misery in our own minds.

What has happened to us? The Bible says that this state of things is due to 'sin'—but what is 'sin'? The great myth of Adam and Eve with which the Bible opens tells us that, from the very beginning, man abused his power of free will by refusing to accept his own limitations. In that myth, the limitation is symbolized by a prohibition against eating an apple —but perhaps that is only a poetic way of putting it. The point of the story is that Man rebelled against the limits set upon him by his created nature; he wanted to have and do what it was not possible for a limited creature to be or do; he wanted to be 'as God'. He was persuaded that there was something that God knew and he did not (which indeed was perfectly true), and he was determined to know it, although he was warned that it was something which Man could not know and live. But he insisted on knowing; and the thing that he chose to know was Evil.

But what was 'Evil'? It was not any created thing; for everything God made was good. Christianity will have nothing to do with those religions which teach that the body is evil, or that matter is evil, or that any existing thing—spirit, mind, or matter—is evil in itself. No; but when man wanted to be 'as God' he got (as our elders used to say of us) 'above himself'. From that god-like elevation he looked (as it were) down on himself and saw himself as he was—limited, dependent, created. And he could not bear it. The creatureliness which should have found its joy in loving obedience, the limitations which should have given him delight in his fellow creatures, the difference between himself and others which should have provided him with happy exchanges of affection—all seemed to him to be hateful and humiliating. Everything he looked on was good, but because of his pride, he could not see it as good—he saw the good as evil.

That is the story of Adam. But it is not the whole story. There is another tradition which has come down to us that tells how something of the same kind had happened earlier and elsewhere in another order of God's creation, one which we do not know very much about: the order of pure spirits, who are created beings with free wills and intelligent minds, but with bodies made of nothing that we should recognize as 'matter'. One of these great and powerful angels also rebelled against his creatureliness, and fell into a rage of misery and frustration, taking many of his fellow angels with him. We cannot, of course, 'prove' the truth of this; but the Lord Christ often spoke as though it was true, so Christians do well to believe it. We call this rebel spirit 'Satan', or 'the Devil', which means 'the enemy'— and that is the right name for him, for he has no friends and there is nothing which he loves: he is the enemy of everybody and everything.

Satan's pride revolted against being a mere dependent creature; he wanted to assert himself and show that he was as great as God. But what could he do? He could not create anything, for all creation belongs to God. The only thing the proud, perverted will can do to assert itself is to destroy. Just as God is one, creative, loving, and real, so the evil power can exercise itself only in division, destruction, hatred, and unreality. God is a Person; but it is scarcely accurate to say that there is a 'personal' Devil, for evil breaks up the personality. Of that proud spirit there is now nothing left but a ravenous, chaotic will, a motiveless and un-meaning malice, at once cunning and witless, like that of a maniac; an empty rage of destructiveness, without hope or purpose save to rend and divide, and reduce all creation to the same hell of futility as itself. It was

to this spirit of strife and destruction that man opened
the doors of his mind when he learned to see God's good
creation as an evil thing. And he opens them to Satan
every time he allows the lust of division and destruction
to take hold of his will; for evil thrives upon division.

Man never fell so far as Satan. His will is split in half,
and that is at once his torment and his hope. The true
creaturely nature is still alive in him. He is still in
touch with reality, still able to love and unite and build
up, still able to reach out to the God whom he has not
wholly rejected. And so far from the body's being the
cause of his fall, we may perhaps think that he is saved
from complete disaster by the humble and blessed flesh
which he shares with the patient animals, and whose
fragility compels him to recognize, in some degree, that
he is a dependent creature, and cannot ever be self-
sufficient. His will is split in half, but it has not fallen
wholly into chaos. Only by the most resolute and determined violence to his own proper nature can a man
bring himself to that final state of disintegration in
which all love, all unity, all constructiveness, and all
sense of reality are dissipated and lost. But that is the
state to which the evil spirit will always try to drive
him, that he may make him 'even such a one as himself'.[1]

Now, we said that the evil spirit throve upon division.
Since evil can create nothing, it can only work its will
by seizing upon some good thing and giving it an ugly
and destructive twist, and the good thing which it thus
distorts to its own end is that variety and *difference*
which, as we have seen, is found in all created beings.
Difference, though it implies limitation, is not evil; it

[1] It is, we believe, possible for a human soul to choose this state,
which we call 'damnation'; but we need not, I feel sure, imagine *persons*
suffering torment for ever in hell. The reality is at once less horrible and
more horrible than that. By the time anybody gets to 'hell', he will have
ceased to be anything that could properly be called a 'person'.

only becomes an occasion of evil when a proud and envious will distorts it into division and hatred. For example: you and I, being human, possess two legs apiece and no more. That, to be sure, is a limitation, but it is not an evil—two legs are the proper number for a human being to get along with. A beetle has six legs; that is his proper number, and they serve him very well, while a worm manages to get along comfortably in spite of the limitation of having no legs at all. Nor is there anything to show that the worm envies the beetle his legs, or that the beetle despises the worm for having none. But when we humans explode into senseless fear and disgust at these creatures because they have fewer or more legs than we have, we are allowing the evil will to seize upon this harmless difference and make it a source of hatred and destruction, so that with cruelty and contempt in our hearts we smash and destroy the beetle and the worm, not because they have injured us, but merely because they are different. We detest, we say, these beastly crawly things. Or again: you are a man and your wife is a woman, and that difference between you is precisely the source of your delight in one another. But it is a difference that can only too easily be twisted into a source of division and misery: if, for example, you fall into a habit of thinking and speaking as though to be different in sex meant necessarily to be in opposition about everything; or if the husband despises the wife for being 'only a woman', or the wife uses her sex to exploit the husband for what money and luxury she can get out of him; or if either of you is possessive and jealous, breaking up the other's friendships or jobs; or if either looks on the other as a mere instrument for comfort or pleasure; or tries to subjugate or 'mould' or in any other way do violence to the other's personality—in these and a hundred other ways the difference of sex may be made into a devil's tool of destructiveness instead of the occasion for what the English Prayer Book calls 'the mutual society, help and comfort that the one ought to have of the other'. Or to take a third example: the fact that one man has a white skin and another a black skin is a variety in the human race that ought to be pleasing and interesting; the fact that one man is an Englishman and another a 'foreigner' ought to mean that each should be able to appreciate and admire the other's qualities all the more because they are different from his own; but the minute we begin to despise and dislike another man, who has offered us no injury, simply and solely because he is 'foreign'—if we start off with a prejudice against him because he is a Jew or a Turk or a South Sea Islander— if we sneeringly sum up all people unlike ourselves as 'niggers, dutchmen, and dagoes'—then we are letting difference become division, and paving the way for 'hatred, malice, and all uncharitableness'; and, even though the nations may be politically at peace, we are waging war in our hearts. Nor does the spirit of evil rest content with putting enmity between man and man, between man and woman, or between man and the brutes; he contrives even to make us enemies of the earth on which we live. He stimulates our avarice and our pride of knowledge so that we look upon the earth as a conquered territory to be exploited, so that we talk of 'wresting the secrets out of nature' (as though 'nature' were an antagonist we had to deal brutally with), and waste the natural resources of coal and oil, tear down forests and create sandy deserts by careless and greedy husbandry, exterminate whole species of plants and animals for gain, turn tracts of fertile soil into slag-heaps and sprawling slums, kill the fish and starve the land by recklessly diverting rain-water from its proper destination, or by pouring chemical refuse into the rivers—thus producing great areas of devastation, which centuries of painful toil will scarcely avail to make good.

'He that is not with me,' said the Lord Christ, 'is against me; and he that gathereth not with me, *scattereth abroad.*' Wherever there is scattering and devastation, there is Satan. Destruction is his hallmark; he cannot create—he can only pull down and tear to pieces; he hates everything that binds people together, everything that builds up and harmonizes, everything that forgets the self in love for something or something other than self; he is, as a great German poet called him, 'the spirit that always negates'—the spirit of nothingness, chaos, and confusion. And by those Dead Sea fruits we may know him.

DOROTHY L. SAYERS

Why do You believe in God and how can It help You?

A SHORT answer to say Why I Believe in God is quick going, and you must do some quick thinking.

First, I am convinced there is a real difference between right and wrong: but I can't make sense of that difference unless there is God. If it's only the way men happen to think that makes things right or wrong, then there is no *real* difference. It's just a matter of preference and social convenience. But some things *are* evil and make men evil: some things *are* good and make men good. I'm sure of that and therefore I'm sure of God.

Second, you and I are Persons. We can stand inside ourselves and look at ourselves. Like animals, we live from moment to moment, doing things: we grow old and die. But we can watch ourselves doing all this, and can pass judgements on ourselves and on the world.

And because of this power we can talk about ideas and ideals, goodness, truth, religion, duty, and death, and can choose death for the sake of something we love more than ourselves. All that takes us into a different kind of world outside time and space. Persons are responsible people—responsible to what? Not *something*, but *someone*. I'm sure of that and therefore I am sure that God, however unlike me, is in some sense a person as I am and you are.

But what about this terrific universe which science reveals to us, a machine complicated beyond belief? Does that leave any room for God? It is far more sensible to suppose that God made it than to think that it made itself! You know there is intelligence in it; we don't put it there: we find it: we can turn nature to our own uses because our minds are not unlike the mind which made it and makes it work. We are part of the machine. But we are outside the machine as well as inside it. We are made in the image of God.

In all kinds of ways then, we reach out beyond this world to something, some Power, mind, goodness we call God. And God speaks back to us, He speaks to us all in Jesus Christ. Christ claimed to know the other end, to have come from it and to have returned to it, to be from God and one with Him. I believe Him. I believe what He tells us about God. I believe in His Resurrection: I think the evidence for it is overwhelming. Christ answers the great questions of men's hearts, Christ makes the world intelligible, and makes evil and suffering tolerable.

I cannot say more of that here. But there's this. There is an infinity of crooked lines: only one kind of line is straight. There are millions of forms of evil. But Good, wherever we meet it, is always the same. Evil destroys —divides: Good creates and unites. We resist evil. We bow the knee to the Good. If evil is the last word in the world, there is no God to help us. It is not: God is. And if God speaks to us all in Christ, He speaks also to each of us in his own heart and conscience, if we will listen.

And now how God can help *you*. But I don't know you, or your job, or your make-up, or the kind of conditions you've got to live in. All I can do is to tell you how belief in God helps me. But that's good enough: for however much you and I may differ, in all essentials we are the same. You and the other fellow and the men who talked to Jesus, we can laugh at the same things, like each other, feel the absurdity and the dignity of life, do each other good or ill; and every man knows that he has but a short time, that he must die, and after that darkness or light. And it is in our essential nature as men that God comes to help us.

How does belief in God help *me*? First, I can look the world in the face. It's not a nightmare, though it sometimes looks like that, nor a futility as some people seem to think. It's got a purpose in it, God's. I can't understand it all. Why should I? God is God, and I am a stupid and a sinful man. But Jesus Christ has made it plain enough that to God people, you and I and the other fellow, matter most—what we make of this life, how we shape for the next. Plenty of people seem to miss the bus, but there *is* a bus to be caught! And it goes somewhere.

Then, I can begin to look other people in the face. They mean something, even if they don't know it, to God. And I can't treat them as though they didn't. Belief in God helps me to understand them, and care about them. We are members of one another, because we all matter to God. It is a duty to love one's neighbour as oneself, even when one does not like him, and Christ shows us what loving him means.

And first and last, I can look myself in the face. If people matter to God, then I do, too, and I've got a responsibility to Him. And once I begin to treat Him like that, He lets me into some of His secrets, and gives to my life a centre, a unity, and a purpose:

1. I get away from myself. Most of the grouses and quarrels and nerves and cruelties of life come from thinking about oneself; God gives one something better to think about—Himself and other people.
2. I know that God wants to do some bit of His work in the world through me. That's fine and the work is worth doing, overcoming my own and other people's evil not by more evil, but with good.
3. I find my own poorness of spirit—that's fine, too, like the soldier who said to our Lord, 'I'm not fit to have you in the same house as me!' That is a

true response to the goodness and majesty of God, and He meets it with a wonderful response of His own.

4. The presence and power of God in my life becomes in Christ a growing reality and that's the finest thing of all. He teaches me to know Him and trust Him in a really personal way.

Perhaps you know all this already. If not, try and see. It begins just by saying, 'Lord, I believe. Help thou my unbelief.'

GEOFFREY CANTUAR:

Why, if God is Love and Almighty, and if He loves every one individually, does He permit such happenings as Earthquakes, causing the awful death of thousands?

I AM always very frank in my answers to these questions. I do not pretend to know more than I do, but I like to try and lay the spectres which are brought up to me; and who shall say that this is not a real spectre which we must face? It was said that more people were made atheists by the earthquake in Lisbon than by any other cause. I will answer this question in four compartments, as it were.

1. First of all, I do not profess to base my belief in the love of God upon anything that I see in the world to-day. I do not pretend to explain, for instance, why some young man is taken away to-day in the prime of life, and an old man of eighty left. No one can live very long in the world without seeing the futility of expecting or of trying to explain things like that. I base my belief in the love of God upon the Incarnation. That I say was a demonstration of love which was meant to last for all time, and in the strength of it, followed by the Resurrection, we were meant to face the trials and difficulties of life. 'Thou must love Me Who hast died for thee.' I have said that in the case of the great mass of mankind the happiness in life outweighs the unhappiness nine to one, which it certainly does; but we wanted this great demonstration of love to hold to in the midst of our trials and difficulties. I do not pretend to find my proof of the love of God in this difficult, perplexed, and very puzzling world as I see it to-day.

2. But, secondly, let us clear our minds of a great mis-understanding. Is the death of two hundred thousand people very different from the death that is going on every day? How many do you think die in London every day? One every eight minutes, day and night. That is about two hundred every day. It would be two hundred thousand, I suppose, in the whole world. And, therefore, are you not making too much of the fact of two hundred thousand dying in one day? Already there are tens of thousands dying. You must ask yourself this: whether you really mean in your mind that the fact of death at all, the fact of these thousands dying every day (earthquake or not) is going to upset your faith in the love of God. Now, death helps my belief in the love of God. The fact of death is increasing human happiness enormously. Suppose there was no death, what would happen? All the people who were living years ago, and are living now, would go on increasing in numbers on this little planet, and growing older, and older, and older, and we should have lost the most beautiful thing in life, the old grand-father and the little child on his knee, the grandmother and her grandchildren around her. We are apt to lose sight of the fact that the great majority of people to-day enjoy life. I should not wish my nearest and dearest to live on when her faculties were gone, and she was too old to enjoy life. Death gives us, and secures to us, our best happiness in life. Do you not remember what Phillips Brooks says: 'God holds the infant like a mother, builds a wall round the strong man, as he fights the noonday battle of his life, and lays the bridge of sunset over which the old man's feet may walk serenely unto the eternal day'?

Death is passing into a sight of even more beautiful things if we have only the faith to believe it. As Canon Holmes quoted beautifully in his book on *Immortality*:

> It is not good that life should know too soon
> The lovely secrets kept for those who die.

Therefore I decline to accept the fact of thousands dying in a day as any evidence against the love of God. He only made us that so many millions of people might sun themselves in the sunshine of His own happiness; and death makes it possible to have so many more millions of people to enjoy life. They have their probation-time here, and if they did not pass away, there would be no room for the thousands of others to come.

3. Then comes the next part of the answer: Why should so many die suddenly? If you had read the geologists' explanation in one of our leading papers at the time, you would have seen the reason why that particular part of the world was so unsafe. It was the last made, the newest bit of earth that has come up and become firm. But we want to answer it not geologically, but theologically. I will tell you what I believe: I believe that all these great things are allowed to happen to prevent us from being drowned in security. We are living, as a matter of fact, upon a quaking jelly, which we call the earth's crust. It is not a solid thing at all. It lasts our time, but only lasts for a time. There is a much greater thing coming than the Messina earthquake—a perfectly inevitable thing—when the earth and all the things therein will be burnt up, when our little planet, struggling away from the sun all the time, but gradually losing its power of keeping away from it, will quite inevitably be drawn into the sun and be burnt up or, according to Sir James Jeans's last book, get farther away and be frozen to death. Our great danger in the world to-day is to have a totally wrong conception of our condition. We want to feel ourselves on solid earth, and to make our homes here. We drift into the idea that this is the place where we ought to be and stay; whereas, as a matter of fact, we are 'strangers and pilgrims on this earth'. What we ought to understand is that if we are found here when the earth is drawn into the sun we shall be burnt up, so far as our bodies are

concerned, with the earth, or frozen to death, if it is the other fate which awaits the earth. The reason, I believe, why God allows these startling calamities to happen on this little earth is to wake us up to a real idea of our condition. Some are simply going on as if they were going to stay here for ever, living as if they were going to live here for the next ten million years. These things wake us up. We live here for a few passing years, and then—this much you and I do know—the world is all done with, so far as we are concerned. That being the case, 'what manner of persons ought we to be', as St. Peter said, 'in all holy conversation and godliness, looking forward and hastening to the coming of the day of the Lord, wherein the heavens being on fire, shall be dissolved, and the elements shall melt with fervent heat?'

I say, then, that while we rush to the rescue of the sufferers, while these great calamities bring out the love and sympathy of the world, let them not move us from our belief in the love of God. Death is no argument against the love of God; but let us take warning ourselves. Are we ready for sudden death ourselves? Are we ready when our turn comes to die?

A. F. LONDON

If God guides Us, how do the Consciences of Christians differ so often, for example, in Politics?

WE have to ask ourselves how God guides people. The idea of guidance is not the same as dominance. We do not imagine that God so completely takes charge of the will and intelligence of the Christian that the person becomes a mere passive instrument in His hands. If that were the case, the acts of a person so dominated would not be his acts at all in any intelligible sense; he would have become a puppet. If we reject this conception of divine guidance, we must think of some way in which the guidance could be given without reducing the person to the status of a mere instrument. This is really not difficult: we can suppose that the grace of God, instead of annulling the faculties of man, makes them keener, raises them to a higher level of efficiency, and, above all, directs them to a worthy end. One of the chief causes of our wrong decisions and blindness to the duties and opportunities which present themselves is our self-centredness. We tend to look at every question from the angle of our own personalities, as if we were the centre of the world. In very subtle ways, therefore, self-interest distorts our judgement. The man who really seeks the guidance of God is taking the first step to overcome the bias of self-centredness and moving towards the true and sane position of God-centredness. But he is only *moving towards* it; he has not fully achieved it. Thus most of us who genuinely desire to be guided by God are still very imperfectly delivered from prejudice. And, of course, the possibilities of self-deception are almost unlimited. We know how often

men have thought that something they desired very
much was the will of God, when all the time they were
simply affirming their own egoism and pride. Not
everyone who claims to be guided by God is really
guided by Him.

Further, we have to draw a distinction between ends
and means. The most important consequence of
becoming a sincere Christian in the sphere of conduct
is that our values for life are changed and we have a
new idea of what purposes we ought to promote. I do
not see how any Christian who is not either a hypocrite
or a very foolish person can fail to see the implications
of Christ's law of love. We cannot confine this precept
to our personal relations; it extends to the social life of
the community. Thus there can be no serious dis-
agreement about what kind of community we ought to
desire. It will be one in which all persons have the
opportunity to develop their potentialities, bodily,
mental and spiritual, and where the living together in
society is, so far as may be, creative, i.e. where the
development of one person does not hamper or restrain
the development of any of his neighbours but facilitates
it. No doubt the full realization of this ideal cannot be
achieved in this world. There never will be a perfect
society on this earth, but there is no reason why we
should not approximate much more closely to the
ideal than has ever yet been done. Unless we are
blinded by self-interest, we shall see that we ought to
promote progress towards the Kingdom of God by all
the means in our power.

By what means? Here the source of differences
between good and sincere men may often be found.
Obviously, my friend and I may both want to go to the
same place but may have quite different opinions about
the best way of getting there. This is true, I think, in
the sphere of political action. Without disagreeing

fundamentally on what we should regard as a good society we may differ profoundly on the next steps. And here, probably, temperament plays its part. Some of us have a sanguine disposition. We don't think much about the risks; we imagine that things will turn out pretty well if we go straight for the goal. But others see the dangers very clearly. They are of the realistic or even pessimistic type, and they believe that society may run down into barbarism or disrupt unless the changes are slow and carefully considered. They have too little belief in the essential goodness of mankind. Of course I have been describing extreme types. There are all kinds between the two extremes. But surely it is evident that good and intelligent men may disagree on the practical questions of politics because they estimate the actual situation differently.

But, you may say, what then is the use of relying on the guidance of God? There is an answer to this. The really devastating and destructive conflicts of opinion in politics and elsewhere are those in which men are not really capable of judging the issue, because motives like self-interest, pride, self-assertion, and sectional loyalties distort their minds. If there were a nation in which the majority of citizens were whole-hearted in their prayer for the guidance of God—and knew what they meant by it—there would still be differences of opinion and probably parties, but every one would agree on the values which matter and would be eager to be enlightened, ready to learn from others, so that there would be no bitter faction. In the discussions of such men the truth would be brought out and the wise policy found. It seems to me that only in so far as there is some element in a society which acts like this can the society grow or even, in the long run, exist.

God, as I see it, does not put the right ideas into our heads, but if we are in communion with Him, He purifies our minds and motives so that we are able to arrive at the right ideas through the faculties which He has given us.

This does not mean that 'waiting upon God' is useless. Some people seem to suppose that if they say a prayer and then make their minds a blank the first notion that occurs to them is the guidance of the Spirit. This, I believe, is dangerous nonsense. We have to use our minds and think as hard as we can. Then, when we have worked at the problem and perhaps are still uncertain what we ought to do, it is well to be quiet and still in the presence of God. When we are prepared and ready to hear, the word of God may come to us clearing up our perplexities.

There is one further consideration. The ultimate purpose of God is evidently so complex and so far beyond our comprehension that we can understand at the most what His will may be for us. We cannot be sure that the purpose of God does not involve what appear to us contradictions, so that the conflict between two honest men who see their public duty differently may be, in the end, better than their agreement.

W. R. MATTHEWS

Does God really take any Notice of Our Prayers?

THERE are two kinds of people in the world, those who believe in prayer and those who do not. Those who do not believe in it as a rule argue that they have given it up, because it does not work. No doubt, in their case, they are right. They have made requests which have not been answered. But it does not seem to have occurred to them that if they had made different requests they might have been answered. The following story will make this point clear.

There was once a man who had three sons. The eldest of them came to him and said: 'Dad, please give me a shilling. I think I have "spotted a winner" and I want to put a bob on it.' His father shook his head. Then the second son came in and said: 'Dad, please give me a shilling.' 'What do you want it for, my boy?' said his father. 'I want to buy some sweets.' 'And what are you going to do with them?' 'Why, eat them of course,' the boy replied. 'What? all of them?' 'Yes, all of them,' said the boy. The father again shook his head. After a time the youngest son came running into the room, and said: 'Dad, do please give me a shilling.' 'Why do you want it?' said his father. 'I want to buy a present for Tommy Brown. He has had an accident and broken his leg.' With a kindly smile the father pulled out the money and gave it to him. 'Ye ask and ye receive not, because ye ask amiss, that ye may spend it in your (selfish) pleasures,' says St. James in his epistle.

When people accuse God of not taking any notice of our prayers, they overlook the great danger of unwise giving, which in human life is far too common. A great many parents, for example, 'spoil' their children by always giving them what they want. God never does that. If God (who is all-powerful) always gave us what we asked, the result would be simply disastrous. Under those circumstances, no wise person would ever dare to ask God for anything, lest it might prove to be his undoing.

We read in the Bible that the two sons of Zebedee came to our Lord and said, 'Master, we would that thou shouldst do for us whatsoever we shall ask of Thee. . . . Grant that we may sit, one on Thy right hand, and one on Thy left hand in Thy glory.' Our Lord's reply was, 'Ye know not what ye ask.' Indeed they did not. Our Lord's throne was a cross, 'and with Him they crucified two thieves, one on his right hand and the other on his left'.

But if God does not give what people ask, but only what is best for them, why, then, does He trouble them to ask at all? Why does He not simply give them what is best for them, and have done with it? To this question it is not very difficult to find the answer. It is found in that often quoted, and often misunderstood, saying: 'Heaven helps those that help themselves.' This, rightly inter-preted, means that God has no use for laziness. He expects men to work for what they receive. Thus, for example, God might have made the world so that the fruits of the earth dropped into man's lap without any effort on his part. This is not the case. Man has to eat bread in the sweat of his brow. He has to work for what he gets, and one form of that work is prayer. In prayer we co-operate with God. In so doing, our characters develop, and we gain increasing insight into the mind of God. In this way we become fitted gradually to receive God's best gifts, which He is waiting to give us. This, at any rate, is the experience of those who persevere in prayer.

But it is important to remember that there is a right

and a wrong way of co-operating with God. It is *His* will and not our own that we are seeking to carry out. Many people make the disastrous mistake of supposing that prayer is an attempt to change the will of God. The will of God, however, is the best thing in the world. Nobody in his senses would think of trying to change it. We pray not in order to change it, but to range ourselves on the side of it. 'Our wills are ours to make them thine.' All prayer, therefore, should be unselfish and God-centred. That is the meaning of the ending 'Through Jesus Christ our Lord'. This is not a magical formula which will ensure our getting what we ask. We use it at the end of our prayers in order to show that we have honestly tried to pray such prayers as Christ would approve. Hence we can dare 'to use His name'.

It follows from this that we should never forget the most unselfish of all forms of prayer, namely intercession, or prayer for others. The Lord's Prayer teaches us not to say 'my' and 'me' but 'our' and 'us'. Especially should we pray for our friends. If we wish to be true friends we owe it to them that we regularly remember them in this way, particularly if they are the kind of people who need help in matters of religion, as so many do. In this way we shall confer upon them the greatest blessing in the world, and that is the blessing of a Christian friendship. While all friendship is good, there is no friendship to equal that.

So far we have spoken of prayer as if it consisted only in asking for things. But, of course, it is far more than that. Obviously, this must be so, if God is our Father. No self-respecting son would approach his father only when he wanted to get something out of him, though there are a good many people who treat their Heavenly Father so. Let us not be like them. We shall often approach Him in prayer in order to thank Him, and also to talk to Him about what is in our hearts. At times we shall be content to kneel in silence before Him, waiting for Him to speak to us. The more we get to know God, the less will our prayers be a string of petitions, and the more will they be like a conversation with a friend. We shall not then be in any doubt that God listens to our prayers. We shall be convinced of it from our own experiences. That is the only way in which we can be convinced.

Let us sum up. If we want to know whether God takes any notice of our prayers, we can only find the answer in one way, by experience. But we must pray in the right way. We must not be selfish in our prayers, but rather seek always to make them pleasing to Him. And we must persevere. Many people give up just when a little more patience and perseverance would have saved the situation. *Never give up your private prayers.*

LINDSAY DEWAR

How can God be Watching over Every One and Listening to Every One's Prayers at Once?

THE difficulty is that we are taught, quite rightly, to think of God as our Father, and to go to Him in prayer as simply as if we were children speaking to their father. That is, we are encouraged to think of God as an individual. If we do not quite picture Him as Blake did or as the medieval pictures do, as an elderly man with a long beard sitting on a throne in heaven, we still feel that if He is a person He must be 'somewhere' rather than everywhere, and only able to attend to a certain number of things at the same time.

Then when we realize that He is the creator of the Universe, of the vastness of starry space, and try to imagine what that means, our belief in Him as our Father becomes very different. When we are told that 'nearer is He than breathing and closer than hands and feet', we may try to believe it, but we can't understand how He can be at once infinite and present with each of us. Our whole idea of a person is bound up with the idea of a particular individual living in a special place at a special time; and our imaginations cannot conceive of a Being who is always and everywhere present, as God must be if He is watching over and listening to every one of His children.

The trouble is that we have to think in images that are borrowed from our own experience in space and time. If, as many of us believe, our deepest experience of communion with God is a consciousness of Him that takes us out of space and time, yet this foretaste of eternity cannot be described in words or pictures or even, I think, in music. The 'moment one and infinite' in which, as St. Paul says, we were 'caught up into the heavenlies' may be a real admission into a realm of existence unlimited by space and time: but if so we cannot translate its meaning into concepts that we can understand or depict.

Of course God must be infinite, in the sense that there can be nothing outside Him, and omnipresent, in the sense that He cannot be absent from any part of His Universe. 'In Him we live and move and have our being.' He isn't a person in the sense of an individual, or indeed a person like a vastly magnified human being. But that does not mean that He is *less* than a person, less able to watch over us or to listen to us.

We have to realize that we can only think of God in the terms of the highest things that we as men know. The highest and holiest things in our experience are persons. A person is higher than what is called a 'value' (beauty, truth, and goodness are values and they all derive their meaning because they are values for, of, or in a person); higher than an abstraction like the life-force or energy; higher than any mere thing. So we are right in thinking of God as a person: it is the best we can do. But it doesn't go far enough, because we cannot think of a person except as we know it in ourselves. God is a person but not a limited individual. He is personal or super-personal, *more* than a person, but not *less*.

Can you grasp what that means? A person, but not confined as we are to a tiny range of interests and activities; a person whose love is not restricted to a particular family or nation or to special places and times; a person infinite in the range of His being, as all-pervading as space itself; a person who cares for all His universe, who is as near and as necessary as the atmosphere, as creative and real as the sun; a person in whom you and I live just as the millions of blood corpuscles in our veins or of living cells in our bodies live in us. Use whatever comparison helps you most: the reality of God will always be far beyond it.

But can so vast a Being care for each of us? Can He really hear and answer? Surely love is always for a particular person at a particular time, always partial and selective. Is it? Of course your love and mine is; but don't we realize that the limits of our love are defects, and due to our own limited capacities? When Plato said that the love of the one leads on to the love of the many, and the love of the many leads on to the love of the all, he was speaking what we know to be true; for love ought always to be growing and expanding; otherwise it is only a form of selfishness. Some of you will have seen a picture, a very excellent picture, in *Punch*, of all places, a picture of a mother surrounded by a dozen people, all the members of her household, each shouting a question at her: she sits there and answers them all. Extend that picture: imagine the largest human love carried on without limit; and you will have the answer to our question.

Can we extend the range of love and not destroy its quality? Surely to love everybody is almost the same as to love nobody. A general benevolence isn't love: for love cares passionately for a particular person, for all his little peculiarities, for what makes him different from others. This universally diffused love must lack the warmth and intimacy that we want to feel when we pray. I don't want a vast all-pervading, undiscriminating Deity but some one who is, if you like, small enough to reach my level, some one who is in a real sense 'my God'.

How much of that feeling is really selfish, a desire to appropriate for myself something that others cannot share, a jealous wish to keep God as my own? Is love at its best possessive and exclusive? Can we, if we really love God, want Him to be 'my God but not yours'?

We shall see an answer to that difficulty if we look at Jesus. No one ever had a stronger sense of the importance and the uniqueness of each separate person. Of all those who came to Him He treated every one as a distinct individual with special character and needs and temptations and capacities. He *cared* for them all with a sympathy and a wisdom and a power of self-giving that is love in its perfection. Yet His love is free from all sentimentality and from all exclusiveness, given to Zacchaeus the publican as freely as to Simon Peter, to the rich young ruler, and to the woman that was a sinner. There is nothing superficial or diffused about it: rather it is searching, discriminating, regenerative, the sort of love that forgives and cures and inspires. And yet Jesus more plainly than any other insisted that God cared for all men, indeed for the hairs of men's heads, and for the two sparrows sold for a farthing; and insisted too that God's love was given like His sunshine to the good and to the evil, to the just and to the unjust. He at least did not feel that the majesty and universality of God made Him less able to watch over and listen to each one of us.

And in this question of ours we can take the lessons of Jesus as true. Don't hesitate to think about God as present everywhere and to believe that 'in Him we, all of us, live and move and have our being'. But don't hesitate to go to Him as simply and directly as Jesus did; and you will find as you do so that you are certainly praying to one who listens and are certainly protected by one who watches. God is like Jesus—that is the central belief of Christianity. The God of the stellar universe, the God who creates and sustains all that is, has been made near to us in Jesus. The quality of Jesus is the quality of God. If that be true, we cannot doubt that He watches over us all, and listens to every prayer.

CHARLES E. RAVEN

What was Christ's Position as God, if He prayed to God?

WE can answer the question, in the form in which it is stated, thus: When Jesus prayed to God, His position as God was that He was God the Son, in the manhood which He had taken, praying to God the Father, and that Father and Son, with the Holy Spirit, are the one sole and supreme God, within Whose being love thus finds its supreme expression. For God is love.

But Christians did not learn this language of theology all at once. It was about four hundred years before the doctrines of the Trinity and the Incarnation were worked out into a form which was satisfactory. In the days when Jesus lived with his fisherman-friends in Galilee, these careful doctrinal phrases had not been invented. The little circle of His followers knew Him as a man, and knew Him with a close intimacy which makes their testimony to His purity of motive and of living, to His love and His courage, to His sureness of touch when He dealt with sin or with sickness, both remarkable and convincing. It was unquestionably a human life in every way, with all the difficulties and responsibilities and temptations that men have to face. And we know that He did not find temptation easy to meet. The struggle in the wilderness after His baptism was long and hard. The agony in the Garden of Gethsemane, when all His human nature shrank from the tragic strain of betrayal and crucifixion, was even harder. Yet He never failed, as we all fail. He won His victory, and won it as a man, and so He won it for us.

But prayer is a natural part of human life. It has been said that 'man is a praying animal'. Certainly it is true that always and everywhere men have prayed to the gods that they knew. And even those who have ceased to believe in God, and who call themselves atheists, have often found themselves, in time of great happiness, or of great need, wanting to cry out, either in praise and thanksgiving, or in longing and entreaty, to the Unseen, whom they do not know. It is thus that Mr. Bertrand Russell, one of the most distinguished scholars and writers of our time, who finds himself utterly unable to believe in God as Christians believe in Him, can yet write of 'A free man's worship'.

What do we know about the prayers of Jesus? It is clear enough that He prayed regularly, and we are told that it was His custom to go to the synagogue and to join in the regular services there, with their beautiful prayers drawn from the Old Testament. Sometimes He would try to escape from the crowds that followed Him everywhere, and to go away to the top of some hill where He could be quiet and pray. On one occasion at least He rose very early in the morning in order to pray. And He told His followers to pray at all times, and to pray persistently. When He was in sore distress, in the Garden of Gethsemane, He sought for a solitary place where He could face the last great crisis of His mission in prayer. In all this He prayed as men pray, and if this had been all, we could have said of Him that He was such an one as are the saints of every religion. But there was something more, something so striking that it has changed man's idea of prayer for all time.

Can we see just what this was, this special mark or note in His praying which led His disciples to ask Him to teach them His own way of prayer? The disciples were already religious men. They were accustomed to the worship of the synagogue, and some at least of them had been followers of John the Baptist, who, as they told Jesus, had taught his disciples his own way of prayer. Why did they want anything more of Jesus? We can see the answer in the teaching about prayer which Jesus gave them, teaching so familiar to us now that we find it hard to realize how new and striking it was. And we must remember that this teaching puts into words for them and for us the actual prayer of Jesus Himself.

In the first place, He taught them to pray to the Father with quite astonishing directness and simplicity. St. Luke has preserved for us what seems to be the earliest form of the Lord's Prayer, and it begins, perfectly naturally, and almost intimately, 'Father, hallowed be Thy name'. But this was just the way in which He prayed Himself. In speaking to God He could speak as though there were no barriers at all. He could come when He would and talk freely, as a child can come to a loving and understanding father or mother. Indeed He spoke to God even more freely, since no father or mother understands as fully as God understands. But this was something quite new, quite unlike the straining after God to which man had been accustomed. Some of His enemies said, in astonishment, that He talked 'as though God were His own Father, putting Himself on a level with God'. And thinking it all over afterwards, that is exactly the claim which the disciples made for Him.

In the second place He spoke of prayer as quite certain to be heard and answered. 'Ask and ye shall receive; seek and ye shall find; knock and it shall be opened unto you. For every one that asketh, receiveth; and he that seeketh, findeth; and to him that knocketh it shall be opened.' We may not always receive exactly what we ask, for we do not always know what is best, for others or for ourselves. But the giving of God is better and not worse than that of an earthly father. 'If ye, being evil, know how to give good gifts unto your children, how much more shall your heavenly Father give the Holy Spirit to them that ask Him.' And so He Himself prayed as one perfectly sure not only that He was heard, but that He was answered. Even in Gethsemane He did not need many words. He laid His need before the Father, wholly ready to accept the Father's will for Him, whatever that will might be: 'If this cup may not pass from Me except I drink it, Thy will be done.'

In such prayer as this men saw what perfect prayer might be. But that meant that they saw God as He really is, wholly loving in His Fatherhood, and that they saw in Jesus One who knew and had shown them the way to God. Thus they came to think of Jesus as One who, though He was so truly and fully man, was more than any man that had ever lived, for He had opened up the way for which men had always been seeking. Through Him they had learned the way up to God Himself. And so at last they came to see that Jesus had done something that only God can do, for it could only be by God's own act that God is made known. What else then could Jesus be save God Himself, revealing in manhood both the truth of God and the truth of man? He could not have been so wholly and perfectly all that man at his highest might be, if God had not acted. And so, as St. John put it, 'In the beginning was the Word, and the Word was with God, and the Word was God. . . . And the Word was made flesh and dwelt among us, and we beheld His glory, the glory as of the only-begotten of the Father, full of grace and truth.'

And so in the prayers of Jesus, it was as man that He prayed to God the Father. But that prayer revealed a deeper truth still, the truth of that mystery of love within the being of God Himself, wherewith the Father loves the Son, and the Son returns that love, in an eternal response which gives meaning to all our lesser prayers. And that is why we so often end our prayers with the words 'through Jesus Christ our Lord'. Not only has He taught us to pray as He prayed when He lived among us as a man, but now and always, in the eternal unity of the Godhead, 'He ever liveth, to make intercession for us'.

L. W. GRENSTED

If Christ was God, How did God look after the World while Christ was in Palestine?

OUR best way of dealing with this question will be by working it into a kind of dramatic story or dialogue.

The scene is a Mission-House in India, in a village not far from Delhi; and the dialogue takes place about Christmas, 1911. An Indian boy, who is being prepared for Christian Baptism, is talking to the missionary, asking him some questions about Jesus.

Boy. Is the Holy Land, where Jesus lived, a real place on earth?

Missionary. Yes, of course it is. Quite a tiny little country, compared with India. It is the country that we usually call Palestine. Anybody can go and visit it, and see the places where Jesus lived and taught and died. I've been there myself.

Boy. How long did Jesus live there?

Missionary. All his life on earth—or very nearly. That is, more than thirty years.

Boy. But who was looking after the rest of the world all that time?

Missionary. What do you mean by that?

Boy. Well, if Christ was God, how could God be ruling in heaven while He was living as a man in Palestine? And who *was* ruling over the universe during those thirty years?

Missionary. What made you think of that?

Boy. Last Sunday's lesson. It was the Christmas story, about God coming down to earth, and beginning as a little child. And then I thought of King George's visit to India. I saw him here with my own eyes a fortnight ago. And I wondered how he could get away from London, where he has to rule over the British Empire. Who *is* governing the British Empire just now, while King George is away from London and is travelling in India? That was another question I wanted to ask.

Missionary. And what do you think the answer to *that* question is?

Boy. Well, I said to myself that, after all, India is *part of* the British Empire. That is why King George has come. While he is in India, he is not *away* from his Empire, or neglecting it, but the very opposite. He has come to help this bit of his Empire. His visit to India is part of his governing the Empire.

Missionary. And doesn't that help to answer your question about God and Christ and Palestine?

Boy. No, I don't think so.

Missionary. Doesn't it? Isn't Palestine part of God's Empire? Of course it is. Though it is a country on earth, that we can go and see for ourselves, it isn't outside of God's Empire. Earth as well as heaven belongs to God. And when Jesus lived in Palestine, that was God coming to the part of His Empire, or His universe, which we call the earth.

Boy. But what about the other parts, all those thirty years? What about His throne in heaven, where He reigns and rules over all? I suppose it's easy for King George, because he will only be away from London for a few months.

Missionary. Yes, and while he is looking after this part of his Empire, in India, other people can carry on the work of government for him in London. It doesn't all depend on him alone. He has plenty of good counsellors in London to help him, and when he travels abroad he can leave the government in their hands for a little.

Boy. And could God do that too?

Missionary. No, God could never do that. That is quite different. God governs every little bit of His universe all the time, and it couldn't go on for one moment without Him.

Boy. But how can that be true if Jesus was God? Surely Jesus wasn't really governing the whole universe while He lived in Palestine. How *could* He, when He was a boy, and especially when He was a baby lying in a manger, as we were told in the Christmas story last Sunday?

Missionary. No, of course He couldn't. I'll try to explain it, though this is the most difficult part of all. . . . When Christians say that Jesus was God, they don't mean that He was just simply altogether God, and that there is no more to be said. It isn't quite as simple as that. It is much deeper. When King George was here a fortnight ago, if somebody had seen him passing, and asked me, 'Who is that?', I should have answered, 'That is King George'. But if when Jesus was in Palestine somebody had seen him passing, and pointed, and asked, 'What man is that?', it would not have been correct to answer, 'That is not a man; that is God'. That couldn't be right. For remember, Jesus used to talk to the people *about* God, and He used to pray *to* God (so the Bible tells us). And remember also, Jesus was crucified and died on the cross, but it would be all wrong to say that *God* was crucified or died on the cross. The followers of Jesus never said that. They knew that Jesus really was a man. But they knew also that He was different from all other men. So they said that He was the Son of God, and they were right. He was a real man, but He was also the Son of God. Or His followers sometimes put it in this other way. It was God the Father that created us, but it was God the Son that came to earth, as a man, in Jesus, to do His Father's will for our salvation.

Boy. Does that mean that God did not come to earth Himself, but sent His Son instead? As if King George, instead of coming to India himself, had sent the Prince of Wales. But it is far better to have the King himself. And

I think it would be far better to have God Himself. Why didn't God come Himself to save us? Why did He only send His Son?

Missionary. Well, that is not quite the right way to put it. It isn't really just like the King sending the Prince. It is quite different when it is God we are speaking of. When we say God sent His Son, it doesn't mean that God the Son came to earth and God the Father stayed behind in heaven. That would sound as if there were two separate Gods. That can't be right, for there is only one God.

Boy. But then how could He be ruling on His throne in heaven while Christ was in Palestine?

Missionary. Well, here is another thing you have to learn. God does not live in a place called heaven far away beyond the sky. We do sometimes picture it like that, and talk about it like that, to make it easier for our minds, and especially for the minds of children. But that is only a childish way of speaking, a sort of picture-thinking. God is much more wonderful than that, and heaven is more wonderful than that too. *Really* heaven is not far away, but very near us, as we sometimes feel when we think of dear friends of ours who have died and gone to heaven. And God is always near us. Wherever we go, we don't really leave God behind. That is true even of ordinary people like ourselves, who are not worthy of God's presence at all. And in a far deeper way it is true of Christ, the Son of God. When He came to earth, He didn't leave God behind. God was not only near Him, not only with Him, but *in* Him. This was God's own way of coming to earth for the salvation of mankind —coming right into human life, to live the life of a real man in this world as *we* have to do. That is what God did in Jesus. Jesus began as a baby, as we always remember at Christmas-time, and then he grew into a boy, and then into a man. And all the time, even when He died on the cross, God was in Him. It all happened in Palestine.

But all the time God was ruling the whole universe too. God was in Christ, but at the same time He was in heaven.

Boy. Do you mean that, while God was in Christ, that was not all there was of God? It wasn't the whole of God, but only part of Him. God was doing other things too, He was in other places too, carrying on His government of the whole world. Is that it?

Missionary. You *might* put it like that. But it isn't quite right to say 'part of God'. God is not made up of parts, that could be in different places. God is a Spirit, and He is independent of space. He doesn't really move from one place to another. He is not confined to *places* at all. He is everywhere, in heaven and earth and all the universe. But He was in Jesus in a quite special way. In Jesus He came right into our human life. So we can see Him in Jesus, and know what He is like. It is true that we can't see the *whole* of God in Jesus. We men and women could never understand the whole of God anyway. But all of God that *could* come into human life *did* come in Jesus. And so when we say that God sent His Son for our salvation, we don't mean that God Himself stayed behind. He wasn't doing less than He *might* have done. It was His very best. It was God Himself that was in Christ in Palestine. And all the time He was ruling His whole universe too. When we think of God creating and governing His universe, we say: 'I believe in God the Father Almighty, Maker of heaven and earth.' When we think of God coming to us in Jesus, in the country called Palestine, nineteen centuries ago, we say: 'I believe in Jesus Christ His Only Son, our Lord, who . . . suffered under Pontius Pilate . . .' And yet these aren't two different Gods, but one God. Now, does all that help you to answer your question?

Boy. Yes, it helps. I had been thinking of God as a King sitting on a real golden throne in a *place* called heaven far away beyond the stars, watching the world from a distance, governing it from above; and I couldn't understand who took His place when He left His throne in heaven and came to earth. Now I understand that it wasn't a case of leaving a throne empty. He came in Jesus Christ His Son, who lived in Palestine, but all the time He was ruling the whole world too. . . . But even then, isn't it difficult to understand how God Almighty could really be in Jesus, as a baby, and as a boy, and as a man, and when He died on the cross, and at the same time be ruling the whole universe as Almighty God?

Missionary. Yes, of course it is difficult to understand. Ever since Jesus lived, His people have been wondering about it, and the very wisest of them have been trying to understand it and to think it out. I don't think anybody can quite explain it. But remember it is GOD we are talking about. It isn't any one else, but God, that could do all that. God could do it. We can't understand it. But God would not be anything like as wonderful to us as He is if we could understand everything He does. It is far better to have a God whom we *can't* altogether understand, isn't it, if only we can understand enough of Him for us to be able to trust Him? And that is just what we can do. He has shown us enough in Jesus Christ. And the more we trust, the more we shall understand.

DONALD M. BAILLIE

Can you Prove that Jesus Lived: Historically?

I HAVE been asked to write something in answer to this question. The first thing I should say is 'What kind of proof do you want?' If you want the sort of proof you can have for a mathematical truth, or for a scientific law which can be submitted to experiment, you can't have that kind of proof for any historical event. You can invent, if you have sufficient ingenuity, a theory to account for the documents relating to any character in history on the supposition that the person never really lived, a theory which does not involve any sheer physical impossibility, even if it involves wild improbabilities. Archbishop Whately wrote in 1819 a skit entitled *Historic Doubts relating to Napoleon Buonaparte*, in which he showed that this could be done even in regard to a famous man still alive. Historical proof is a matter of greater or less probability, and when you come to estimate what is probable, in view of the documentary evidence, it is the judgement of the person who is familiar with that particular field which counts. Anybody who has not had the opportunity of studying that field may come up against arguments making out that something is probable which an expert, who does know the field, can see to be worth nothing.

No one would ever raise the question 'Can you prove that Jesus lived?' unless there had been people who claimed to show that it was improbable that He ever lived. Now anybody who hears an anti-Christian lecturer at a street corner declare that the documentary evidence makes it improbable that Jesus ever lived, can't hope to judge by his own untrained judgement what is probable or improbable in regard to documents of nineteen hundred years ago. He has to take as probable what the body of scholarly opinion regards as probable, and thus he is impressed by the lecturer's statement, so far as he believes that the body of scholarly opinion supports the view that Jesus never lived. If that is what the lecturer tries to make his audience believe, he is either ignorant himself of what scholarly opinion as a whole really is, or he is consciously imposing upon his hearers' credulity. There have, it is true, been a few writers in recent times, though not scholars of the highest rank, who have maintained that Jesus never lived, but all those recognized as the chief authorities in this part of ancient history have treated such a view as utterly absurd. It has never been the view of more than a few cranks, like the view that Bacon wrote Shakespeare. If it was only Christians who maintained that Jesus lived, you might say that their judgement was warped by their pre-conceived belief, and so I point to two men who have written from a standpoint quite apart from the Christian one, and stand in the first rank as authorities on ancient history. One is the great German historian, Eduard Meyer, who died the other day, the chief ancient historian of our time. One of his latest books was a history of the origins of Christianity, and not only did he believe that Jesus was a real man in history, but he put a high value upon our Gospels as historical documents showing what Jesus was like. The second man is Sir James Frazer, whose special subject is those worships of mythical saviour gods on which people who try to make the story of Jesus mythical mainly build. What does Sir James Frazer himself say?

'The doubts which have been cast on the historical reality of Jesus are, in my judgment, *unworthy of serious attention*. Quite apart from the positive evidence of history and tradition, the origin of a great religious and moral reform is inexplicable without the personal existence of a great Reformer.

To dissolve the Founder of Christianity into a myth, as some would do, is hardly less absurd than it would be to do the same for Mohammed, Luther, and Calvin. Such dissolving views are for the most part the dreams of students who know the great world chiefly through its pale reflection in books.'[1]

One may give an example how an argument which may seem strong to some one who does not know the facts is really worthless. A great deal is made by street-corner lecturers of the fact that in all the Greek and Roman writings coming down from the first century, other than the writings of Christians, there is no mention of Jesus. That may be quite true, but the argument leaves out of account that what we possess to-day of the writings of the first century are mere scraps and relics, and that those who wrote for the educated Greek and Roman public would have thought it below the dignity of history to notice the doings and sayings of a wandering preacher among one of the conquered peoples of the Empire. What they wrote about was wars and politics and the doings of emperors and kings. Let us think of a modern analogy. Suppose that all the printed writing of to-day had perished, except Mr. Winston Churchill's *History of the World War*, Mr. Bernard Shaw's books, and some hundred odd issues of *The Morning Post*. What mention would one find in these writings of the Sadhu Sundar Singh? Who, you ask, was the Sadhu Sundar Singh? Well, there you are! You don't know of him, any more than thousands of people in the Roman world of the first century knew about Jesus, and yet the Sadhu has been a very real man of our time. Multitudes in India have regarded him with reverence; many men have followed him. Miraculous stories have been connected with him. If, in some future age, a book about the Sadhu[2] happened to survive

---

[1] *The Golden Bough*, pt. vi, p. 412.
[2] See *The Sadhu*, by Canon B. H. Streeter and A. J. Appasamy. Macmillan & Co.

alongside of the other writings just mentioned, would it be reasonable to say that the Sadhu Sundar Singh was a myth because there was no mention of him in Mr. Winston Churchill's *History of the World War* or Mr. Bernard Shaw's books or in the hundred odd numbers of *The Morning Post*?

There is one misunderstanding which must be guarded against. If historical evidence can never yield more than greater or less probability, does belief in Jesus, it may be asked, stand on a mere probability, and that a probability the strength of which can be estimated only by experts accustomed to deal with a particular class of documents? The answer to this question might be Yes, if Jesus were a character in past history and nothing more. If there had never been any Christian Church, and to-day we discovered the Gospels in some old library, we might have no more than a probability that the Person shown in these books had really lived among men. But Jesus is much more than a character in past history. He has been continuously active in the society of men called His 'Church'. Men throughout the ages have been in contact with Jesus as a living Person. Thus for those whom Jesus saves what might otherwise be only an historical probability becomes a certainty of faith.

EDWYN BEVAN

What are We to make of
Jesus Christ?

'WHAT are we to make of Jesus Christ?' This is a question which has, in a sense, a frantically comic side. For the real question is not what are we to make of Christ, but what is He to make of us? The picture of a fly sitting deciding what it is going to make of an elephant has comic elements about it. But perhaps the questioner meant what are we to make of Him in the sense of 'How are we to solve the historical problem set us by the recorded sayings and acts of this Man?' This problem is to reconcile two things. On the one hand you have got the almost generally admitted depth and sanity of His moral teaching, which is not very seriously questioned, even by those who are opposed to Christianity. In fact, I find when I am arguing with very anti-God people that they rather make a point of saying, 'I am entirely in favour of the moral teaching of Christianity'—and there seems to be a general agreement that in the teaching of this Man and of His immediate followers, moral truth is exhibited at its purest and best. It is not sloppy idealism, it is full of wisdom and shrewdness. The whole thing is realistic, fresh to the highest degree, the product of a sane mind. That is one phenomenon.

The other phenomenon is the quite appalling nature of this Man's theological remarks. You all know what I mean, and I want rather to stress the point that the appalling claim which this Man seems to be making is not merely made at one moment of His career. There is, of course, the one moment which led to His execution. The moment at which the High Priest said to

Him, 'Who are you?' 'I am the Anointed, the Son of the uncreated God, and you shall see Me appearing at the end of all history as the judge of the Universe.' But that claim, in fact, does not rest on this one dramatic moment. When you look into His conversation you will find this sort of claim running through the whole thing. For instance, He went about saying to people, 'I forgive your sins.' Now it is quite natural for a man to forgive something you do to *him*. Thus if somebody cheats *me* out of £5 it is quite possible and reasonable for me to say, 'Well, I forgive them, we will say no more about it.' What on earth would you say if somebody had done *you* out of £5 and *I* said, 'That is all right, I forgive him'? Then there is a curious thing which seems to slip out almost by accident. On one occasion this Man is sitting looking down on Jerusalem from the hill above it and suddenly in comes an extraordinary remark—'I keep on sending you prophets and wise men.' Nobody comments on it. And yet, quite suddenly, almost incidentally, He is claiming to be the power that all through the centuries is sending wise men and leaders into the world. Here is another curious remark: in almost every religion there are unpleasant observances like fasting. This Man suddenly remarks one day, 'No one need fast while I am here.' Who is this Man who remarks that His mere presence suspends all normal rules? Who is the person who can suddenly tell the School they can have a half-holiday? Sometimes the statements put forward the assumption that He, the Speaker, is completely without sin or fault. This is always the attitude. 'You, to whom I am talking, are all sinners', and He never remotely suggests that this same reproach can be brought against Him. He says again, 'I am the begotten of the One God, before Abraham was, I am', and remember what the words 'I am' were in Hebrew. They were the name of God, which must not be spoken by any human being, the name which it was death to utter.

Well, that is the other side. On the one side clear, definite moral teaching. On the other, claims, which, if not true, are those of a megalomaniac, compared with whom Hitler was the most sane and humble of men. There is no half-way house and there is no parallel in other religions. If you had gone to Buddha and asked him 'Are you the son of Bramah?' he would have said, 'My son, you are still in the vale of illusion.' If you had gone to Socrates and asked, 'Are you Zeus?' he would have laughed at you. If you had gone to Mohammed and asked, 'Are you Allah?' he would first have rent his clothes and then cut your head off. If you had asked Confucius, 'Are you Heaven?', I think he would have probably replied, 'Remarks which are not in accordance with nature are in bad taste.' The idea of a great moral teacher saying what Christ said is out of the question. In my opinion, the only person who can say that sort of thing is either God or a complete lunatic suffering from that form of delusion which undermines the whole mind of man. If you think you are a poached egg, when you are not looking for a piece of toast to suit you you may be sane, but if you think you are God, there is no chance for you. We may note in passing that He was never regarded as a mere moral teacher. He did not produce that effect on any of the people who actually met Him. He produced mainly three effects—Hatred—Terror—Adoration. There was no trace of people expressing mild approval.

What are we to do about reconciling the two contradictory phenomena? One attempt consists in saying that the Man did not really say these things, but that His followers exaggerated the story, and so the legend grew up that He had said them. This is difficult because His followers were all Jews; that is, they belonged to that Nation which of all others was most convinced that there was only one God—that there could not possibly be another. It is very odd that this horrible invention about a religious leader should grow up among the one people in the whole earth least likely to make such a mistake. On the contrary we get the impression that none of His immediate followers or even of the New Testament writers embraced the doctrine at all easily.

Another point is that on that view you would have to regard the accounts of the Man as being *legends*. Now, as a literary historian, I am perfectly convinced that whatever else the Gospels are they are not legends. I have read a great deal of legend and I am quite clear that they are not the same sort of thing. They are not artistic enough to be legends. From an imaginative point of view they are clumsy, they don't work up to things properly. Most of the life of Jesus is totally unknown to us, as is the life of anyone else who lived at that time, and no people building up a legend would allow that to be so. Apart from bits of the Platonic dialogues, there are no conversations that I know of in ancient literature like the Fourth Gospel. There is nothing, even in modern literature, until about a hundred years ago when the realistic novel came into existence. In the story of the woman taken in adultery we are told Christ bent down and scribbled in the dust with His finger. Nothing comes of this. No one has ever based any doctrine on it. And the art of *inventing* little irrelevant details to make an imaginary scene more convincing is a purely modern art. Surely the only explanation of this passage is that the thing really happened? The author put it in simply because he had *seen* it.

Then we come to the strangest story of all, the story of the Resurrection. It is very necessary to get the story clear. I heard a man say, 'The importance of the Resurrection is that it gives evidence of survival, evidence that the human personality survives death.' On that view what happened to Christ would be what had always happened to all men, the difference being that in Christ's case we were privileged to see it happening. This is certainly not what the earliest Christian writers thought. Something perfectly new in the history of the Universe had happened. Christ had defeated death. The door which had always been locked had for the very first time been forced open. This is something quite distinct from mere ghost-survival. I don't mean that they disbelieved in ghost-survival. On the contrary, they believed in it so firmly that, on more than one occasion, Christ had had to assure them that He was *not* a ghost. The point is that while believing in survival they yet regarded the Resurrection as something totally different and new. The Resurrection narratives are not a picture of survival after death; they record how a totally new mode of being has arisen in the Universe. Something new has appeared in the Universe: as new as the first coming of organic life. This Man, after death, does not get divided into 'ghost' and 'corpse'. A new mode of being has arisen. That is the story. What are we going to make of it?

The question is, I suppose, whether any hypothesis covers the facts so well as the Christian hypothesis. That hypothesis is that God has come down into the created universe, down to manhood—and come up again, pulling it up with Him. The alternative hypothesis is not legend, nor exaggeration, nor the apparitions of a ghost. It is either lunacy or lies. Unless one can take the second alternative (and I can't) one turns to the Christian theory.

'What are we to make of Christ?' There is no question of what we can make of Him, it is entirely a question of what He intends to make of us. You must accept or reject the story.

The things He says are very different from what any other teacher has said. Others say, 'This is the truth about the Universe. This is the way you ought to go', but He says, '*I* am the Truth, and the Way, and the Life.' He says, 'No man can reach absolute reality, except through Me. Try to retain your own life and you will be inevitably ruined. Give yourself away and you will be saved.' He says, 'If you are ashamed of Me, if, when you hear this call, you turn the other way, I also will look the other way when I come again as God without disguise. If anything whatever is keeping you from God and from Me, whatever it is, throw it away. If it is your eye, pull it out. If it is your hand, cut it off. If you put yourself first you will be last. Come to Me everyone who is carrying a heavy load, I will set that right. Your sins, all of them, are wiped out, I can do that. I am Re-birth, I am Life. Eat Me, drink Me, I am your Food. And finally, do not be afraid, I have overcome the whole Universe.' That is the issue.

C. S. LEWIS

Do you need to Believe in the Virgin Birth to be a Christian?

JESUS was not born in the usual way because He was not a usual man. He is the eternal Son of God, truly and fully man, but more than merely *a man*. He is THE MAN, the One who gathered up into union with His divine Person the whole human race. St. Paul says of Him, 'He is before all things, and by Him all things consist' (i.e. stand or hold together).[1] You can't say, without a sense of degradation, 'I live; yet not I, but Mr. Smith lives in me.' You *can* say, with St. Paul, 'I live; yet not I, but Christ liveth in me.'[2] His indwelling is the basis of all human personality. He is the Word of God 'by whom all things were made', 'the true Light which lighteth every man, coming into the world'.[3] Professor Romanes answers your question. George Romanes was Darwin's greatest disciple, and the Regius Professor of Physics in the University of Oxford. He was at first an agnostic, and felt it his duty to write three destructive essays against the Christian religion, because he thought that this doctrine of the Incarnation, that 'the Word became flesh, and dwelt among us' was utterly absurd. But under the influence of Dr. C. Gore and others he learned to doubt his doubts; was converted to the Christian religion; became a devout communicant in the Church; and wrote a complete refutation of his former errors, *Thoughts on Religion*. In it he answers the objection that the Incarnation 'is opposed to common sense'. 'No doubt, utterly so; but so *it ought to be if true*. Common sense is merely a rough register of common experience; but the Incarnation, if it ever took place, whatever else it may

[1] Col. i. 17.   [2] Gal. ii. 20.
[3] John i. 3, 9.

have been, at all events cannot have been a common event' (p. 175).

The belief in the Virgin Birth is *a dependent belief*, dependent on the acceptance of Jesus as the eternal Son of God. If *for other reasons*, such as His sinless life, His character and claims, His teaching, His resurrection, His influence on the world, and your own living experience of His love and friendship, you believe the Church's teaching that He is the eternal Son of God, then it is most congruous that He should enter our human life by a Virgin Birth. This is the way in which the first Christians received it.

Why two earthly Parents? When I myself was troubled about this unusual birth, I analysed my doubts. I asked myself what lay behind my reluctant doubt? Was there some prejudice? Yes, certainly. I was reluctant to express my personal belief in an event which seemed against the ordered sequence of history, an irregular occurrence in the closed-in tidy universe which science had invented. No other case of virgin birth had occurred in the history of the human race; there had always been two earthly parents. Why two parents? This led me to study the facts and meaning of sex. I had always believed that two parents were essential to fertilization and to the reproduction of life. But now I learned that this is not true. Two parents are not in the least necessary to the production of life. When life first appeared on the earth the idea of two parents seems never to have occurred to Nature. Many whole species of living things are reproduced by parthenogenesis, reproduction without sexual union. Nature has used several methods of reproduction: budding, as in the sea-weed and yeast, fission, karyokinesis—the splitting of the nucleus, self-fertilization, alternation. Why, then, did nature introduce differentiation of sex when two cells join together (conjugate) to produce a third? I studied the embryologists, and sum up their opinion in these extracts. In *Embryology*, by Sir Gerald Leighton, p. 12, I read:

'It is important at this stage to note that the creatures we have mentioned, and even some more highly organized, such as an amoeba, which has a nucleus, go through these simple or complicated reproductive processes in the total absence of anything which could suggest a distinction of sex. In these cases the individuals are obviously all of one sex, and therefore the distinction of sexes into male and female is evidently something which has been added later in the scheme of evolution, not for the purpose of reproduction itself, but for something which is to be added to that.'

What is that purpose? I read Sir G. Archdall Reid's *Laws of Heredity* (1910):

'Some species consist only of females. They are parthenogenetic, that is the virgin females produce offspring. Without union with another germ cell the ovum becomes the ancestor of a new cell-community' (p. 2).

'According to this hypothesis, therefore, it would appear that the function of sex is to render nature powerless to reproduce adaptive changes' (p. 320).

'The function of sex is to blend parental characters' (p. 202).

'On the other hand, if, as Mendelians suppose, bi-parental reproduction mixes parental characters as marbles are mixed but leaves them otherwise unchanged, we have *no alternative but to suppose that such mixing is both the effect and the actual function of sex. I think it is impossible to imagine any other function*' (footnote, p. 188). (The italics are mine.)

The general result of my studies was to convince me that the function of sex, the purpose of having two earthly parents, is to give a double set of gametes or genes of inheritance to the new offspring so as to give it a better chance in life. As in the Incarnation of the Son of God there would be no need for this double inheritance, there seems to be no reason whatever why our Lord should have two earthly parents.

G

I do not quote from scientific men to confirm the Christian Faith. Science is working in a different 'universe of discourse', an abstract 'closed-in' universe, and with a technical apparatus which cannot allow God to intervene in His universe as it would upset all their calculations. I only quote the writings of scientific men to show that the deep-seated, violent prejudice against the Virgin Birth has no support whatever from what Science can tell us of God's ways of working in the world. He has used many ways of transmitting life. The method of bi-parentalism was introduced for a purpose which does not apply to the Incarnation. The method of virgin birth *does* apply; and is seen to be most congruous, especially in this respect—that it does not involve any self-regarding impulse.

Christians are born of God, not made by their opinions: born by the virgin birth of 'water and the Spirit' in Holy Baptism,[1] 'born, not of blood, nor of the will of the flesh, nor of the will of man, but of God'.[2] The free act of God's love chose you to be born again into the glorious Family of the Twice-born sons of God. I think the question really means: 'Can you retain full belief in Christ as Son of God without believing in the Virgin Birth?' Many have tried and failed to do so. Professor Orr writes in *The Virgin Birth of Christ*, p. 206: 'The best proof of all of the inadequacy of this half-way position is that, historically, it has never been able to maintain itself.' It is a matter of personal guidance on which a lad should consult his minister or priest. I can only state general principles. If a lad desires with all his heart to believe what the Church teaches, and yet cannot say that he is personally convinced of it, I think that he should remain in the Communion of the Church with the prayer: 'Lord, I believe: help Thou my unbelief.' Your

[1] John iii. 5.   [2] John i. 13.

personal opinion may change from day to day, with every book you read. So it is best to trust the corporate Creed, the Family tradition. There is nothing wrong in doubting, provided you doubt your doubts and know your ignorance. There is nothing wrong in the question: 'How can this be?' In fact that was the very question the Virgin Mary asked when the Angel told her that she should be the mother of the Son of God.[1] But note:

1. *Unquestioning Faith is quite reasonable*, if you do not care to form a personal opinion, accepting it just because your mother, the Church, teaches it. This is the way in which you have accepted another belief of the same kind, without question; the belief that you are the son of him whom you have always regarded as your father. You have accepted this without doubt or question simply on the strength of the family tradition; and would be rather shocked and offended if asked to prove it; which might be impossible if you were an orphan. I only mention this to show you that birth differs from every other event because two persons only can give first-hand testimony. I must refer you for a full discussion of this subject to two books by most competent scholars: *The Virgin Birth of Jesus*, by Dr. G. H. Box (1916), and *The Virgin Birth of our Lord*, by Dr. L. Prestige (1918). From these we learn:

2. *The Evidence.* I think it is as good as it could be, considering the subject and the circumstances. (i) It was recorded as soon as it could be with any decency by St. Luke and by St. Matthew who had the opportunity, knowing what those believed who were in direct touch with the Virgin Mary and St. Joseph, who would have contradicted it at once if it was not true. (ii) Their testimony is reinforced by the slanders of the Jews. (iii) As we have seen, such a birth is most congruous with the

[1] Luke i. 34.

belief about the Person of our Lord, taught by St. John and St. Paul. (iv) Of course it was not mentioned in the preaching because it is a *dependent* belief; and because it could not be discussed publicly before hostile crowds while Mary was alive. You wouldn't like your birth and your mother's character to be discussed in every Church and Chapel while she was alive.

3. *Doubt your Doubts.* Don't accept your doubts on authority. Ask 'Why do I doubt?' Professor Romanes did this, and writes: 'The doctrines of the Incarnation and the Trinity seemed to me most absurd in my agnostic days. But now, as a pure agnostic' (one without prejudices) 'I see no rational difficulty at all.' 'Now at one time it seemed to me impossible that any proposition, verbally intelligible as such, could be more violently absurd than that of the doctrine (of the Incarnation). Now I see that this stand-point is *wholly irrational*, due to the blindness of reason itself promoted by (purely) scientific habits of thought.' What lies behind the reluctance to believe in such a birth? 'It seems to be inconsistent with the ordered universe of science.' But this universe of science is not the *real* universe; it is only an 'abstraction', a section cut off, a model made for working purposes, e.g. the 'billiard-ball' model of matter. In my seventy years of life I have seen three such models created and abandoned; I have attended the birth of three 'Modern Minds': watched them nervously squeezing themselves into the current scientific model: and die. I have attended their funerals; and each has left me something in its will for which I am profoundly grateful! You can't stake your life on two such instabilities as a changing science and a growing mind; this is to build your house on the sands. The real world includes 'judgement-values' such as the Good, the Beautiful, and the True, and 're-lationships', as well as 'existences'. Reason by itself cannot judge the Truth. A merely 'natural' religion is

worthless: it cannot save men. Christianity is essentially 'supernatural'. By 'natural' I mean 'the energizing of those forces which God has implanted in created things'. By 'supernatural' I mean 'the energizing of forces, and the activity of Persons, who are not included in the sum-total of created things'. A God who cannot intervene cannot save. So, while using your reason to satisfy your-self that the evidence is sufficient to justify an adventure of faith, allow your heart to speak: fall down and worship God in the Holy Eucharist: and repeat the ancient hymn, from the liturgy of St. James:

Let all mortal flesh keep silence, and with fear and trembling
    stand;
Ponder nothing earthly-minded, for with blessings in his
    hand,
Christ our God to earth descendeth, our full homage to
    demand.

King of kings, yet born of Mary, as of old on earth He
    stood,
Lord of lords, in human vesture—in the Body and the
    Blood—
He will give to all the faithful His own Self for heavenly
    food.

Rank on rank the host of heaven spreads its vanguard on
    the way,
As the Light of light descendeth from the realms of endless
    day,
That the powers of hell may vanish as the darkness clears
    away.

At His feet the six-winged Seraph; Cherubim with sleepless
    eye,
Veil their faces to the Presence, as with ceaseless voice they
    cry,
Alleluya, Alleluya, Alleluya, Lord most High.

For only to the humble-minded, and in prayer and worship, can the assurance of the Truth be born in your heart by the overshadowing of the Holy Spirit.

PAUL B. BULL, C.R.

Did not Some One have to betray Jesus, to fulfil the Scriptures; so why blame Judas, or for that matter, Pontius Pilate? If Christ had to be Crucified, in what way was His Crucifixion Wrong?

'CHRIST *had* to be crucified.' What do we mean by that? I suggest that what we mean, to start with, is that in a world like this, men being what they are, such a person as Jesus Christ was certain to be made to suffer.

There are various sorts of people in the world—the good, wise, kindly, and honest sort, who are out to help their fellow men, and the crooked, stupid, vicious, and cruel sort who prey upon their fellows for their own ends. So there are bound to be clashes and conflicts. If you see a man of high principles setting out to fight some gross and powerful evil, then, knowing what people are, you say, 'He's in for it.' You do not mean that it is written in some book of fate that he is doomed to suffer such and such things; but that, the world being what it is, he must expect to suffer for his principles. Most of us are such half-and-half people that we manage to avoid the more severe kinds of conflict; but we know that if we really mean to do the right, come what may, we must be prepared to pay the cost; and we know that the man who is 'all out' for high and unpopular ideals must count upon opposition and ill treatment. He rarely escapes.

Four hundred years before Christ a wise Greek thinker, Plato, put this in a challenging way. Suppose, he said, that a man appeared who was completely righteous in every way; and suppose the standards of the community were so false that everything he did seemed to them unrighteous: what would happen to him? He would be hated, abused, and finally crucified. Plato was simply going upon the facts of life as he had observed them, when he said that in a world like this the righteous must suffer.

When the Hebrew prophets, hundreds of years before Christ, drew a picture of the righteous Servant of the Lord, brought 'as a sheep to the slaughter', they were, I think, doing much the same thing that Plato was doing: they were interpreting the facts of life as they saw them, only with a deeper insight even than Plato's. (This insight we call inspiration.) They, too, saw that to keep the law of God in a wicked world brought suffering with it; but they saw also that such suffering might be borne in such a way that it would in the end be a means of bringing the wicked to repentance and to salvation: 'by His stripes we are healed.'

Now Jesus Christ, when he came, fulfilled the ideal set forth by Plato and by the prophets as no one else ever fulfilled it before or since. He embodied in Himself the most perfect righteousness that any one could conceive, and His whole life was perfectly devoted to it. He went about doing good without any of that regard for self which in all of us limits the good that we are prepared to do.

The world into which He came had much evil in it. The good that He did came in conflict with the evil. What was likely to happen? You do not need to be a fatalist to say, 'Christ *had* to suffer.'

But if Christ had to suffer, then somebody or other must be the agent in causing His sufferings, not because they were singled out by fate for this sinister part, but because they were in a position where the line of conduct they chose had direct effects upon Him; and because they were capable of the kind of conduct that caused Him to suffer.

Let us be clear that Pilate and Judas were not alto-

gether bad men, nor even worse men than a great many
of their contemporaries, or of ourselves. Pilate had good
deeds to his credit. (Among other things, he had given
Jerusalem for the first time a really efficient water-
supply.) He was no doubt a stern and harsh governor.
He thought it was his duty to be so. He was responsible
to the Emperor for a rebellious province. Any one can see
that when Jesus was brought before him he tried hard to
do the right thing. He failed because (like many of us) he
had done wrong things in the past which made it ex-
tremely difficult to do the right thing now; and because
(again like many of us) he was just not brave enough to
take the risk. If we look deeply enough, we can see that
his act of injustice (which he saw to be such) was inevitable—not because he was fated so to act, but because
of what he was, and of what he had done in the past. If
all through his life he had been more honest, just, and
brave, less anxious for his own skin and the saving of his
face, he need not have been afraid to do the right now
and take the consequences. But of how many of us could
the same be said?

Judas is a puzzling case. Do you suppose that when he
left all to follow Jesus, like Peter and James and John;
when he shared His toils and trials for so many months—
he was all the time nursing black treachery in his heart?
I do not think so. Judas was capable of fine things. But
there was a bad streak in him. We cannot pretend to
know by what means his mind got so twisted that he
entertained the thought of treachery. But we can be sure
that he must have allowed himself to dwell upon dark
thoughts of his own until he came to feel that the only
thing to do was to betray his Master. He cannot have
done such a thing lightly; and I do not think he did it just
for thirty pieces of silver: it went deeper. He committed
the crime, but there was enough good left in Judas to
bring him to an appalling remorse for what he had done.

The whole thing was horrible; and yet who knows which of us might be capable of such treachery if the temptation were strong enough?

Let us put it in this way: when it came to the point, Pilate and Judas did what they did because of what they were: if they were bound to do it, they were bound only by their own characters and their previous thoughts and actions. If Pilate had been brave and honest, if Judas had been true to his own highest ideals, there was no power that could have made them act so sinister a part.

If they had not played that part, I think we must say that somebody, in some way or other, would have compassed the death of Christ. Things being as they were, the righteous Servant of God must needs suffer. And Pilate and Judas were after all no more than the agents of a great mass of hatred and evil with which Jesus was surrounded—the jealousy of the priests, the fanaticism of the Scribes and Pharisees, the worldly aims of the populace, the violence of the Zealots.

And when we come to think of it, the evil that we condemn in all these people is the evil that is in ourselves. If we blame Pilate and Judas, or those who stood behind them, for the crime of the Crucifixion, we blame ourselves. Supposing you or I had been present on that black Friday: on which side should we have shouted? Knowing what we now know, it is easy to persuade ourselves that we should have stood by Jesus. But if we had done so, we should have been very bright exceptions. Everybody who counted was against Him. Even Peter denied Him, and His own disciples forsook Him and fled. I wonder if we should really have behaved any better.

Now as I see it, one great effect of the death of Christ is just to bring home to us the real nature of the evil things that are in us—like selfishness and pride and prejudice and jealousy and cowardice. These are in us as they were in Pilate and Judas and the rest. In them we see our own sins projected like a moving picture on the screen of history. If we realize that, it shakes us pretty rudely out of any self-satisfaction.

If that were all, then the story of the Cross of Christ would hardly be 'Gospel', that is, good news; it would be very bad news indeed. It is as though the Judge of all the world were putting on the black cap to pronounce our sentence.

But the crime of the Crucifixion is on the other side of it the most magnificent example of self-sacrifice. Jesus went to His death in a way which shows that the evil in the world had no power whatever over His spirit. The suffering of a man is not simply a physical fact (like the suffering of a wild animal): it is also a spiritual fact. And from that point of view the important thing is the way in which the suffering is borne. We have accounts in history of other crucifixions than that of Jesus. In some cases the sufferer employed his last hours in hurling bitter curses at his foes. Jesus prayed for them to the last. And as we look back over His life we see that this was the spirit that was revealed all through it. He lived and died in selfless love for others. All the malice and hatred with which He was met did nothing to diminish that love.

We have seen that Jesus fulfilled in His life and death the prophets' ideal of the righteous Servant of God. But He went a good deal further than any ideal that the prophets had formed. His 'righteousness' was a greater thing than they had conceived: it was selfless love, constantly active for the good of men, bringing healing and forgiveness and the power of a better life. Because of this love for men He could not resent or resist or avenge the wrong they did Him.

When a man suffers wrong in this way, then the suffering which he endures is transformed by his patience, courage, and self-sacrifice into a power for good; not because suffering in itself has that virtue, but because the spirit that suffers in that way has triumphed over the evil. Thus in the death of Christ we see not defeat but victory.

This brings me to a further point. I have been discussing the question in what sense Christ *had* to suffer. Suppose we now put it in another way: did God decree that Christ should suffer, and if so, in what sense?

I suggest the answer: what God designed was not the sufferings which befell Christ: what He designed was the kind of life that Christ lived, and the spirit in which His sufferings were endured. Let me go back to that idea of Plato's, that if a perfectly righteous man should appear, he would be the victim of unrighteous men. Now what God designed was the coming of the perfectly righteous Man. As Plato and the prophets saw, His appearance in the world led to His suffering and death: the world being what it is, that was inevitable. But what God designed was something better than any prophet dreamed. He sent into the world 'the Son of His love'. He sent Christ, who embodied in Himself the spirit of love, which is the most divine thing in the universe; for 'God is love'. And Christ so lived that this divine love found expression in all that He said and did; and when the inevitable suffering came upon Him, which must come upon the good man in a wicked world, the same divine love found expression in His suffering and death.

It is in this sense that the Cross was divinely appointed: not that God designed the outward event, which was the crime of men—the crime of us all; but that God revealed Himself in the spirit that bore the Cross; revealed Himself as love, which offers forgiveness for the crime of men, that is, for the sins of us all.

C. H. DODD

Why did Christ Work Miracles? Did He need to?

SOME of us can remember the time when there were no aeroplanes, no X-rays, no wireless sets. Every invention and every new discovery calls upon our mind to make room for new facts. It was once regarded as quite absurd to suppose that swallows could fly from Africa to this country in the spring and back again in the autumn. It was found easier to believe that they spent the winter buried in the mud of fens and marshes. When the facts of migration were established, men had to make room in their minds for this strange truth, that birds can pilot themselves, on their long journey, by a mysterious, but unerring instinct. We must not lightly say 'Impossible!' It is supposed, in some quarters, that certain people have a peculiar power, by which they are able to make cups and jars and other solid things float in the air. If this is proved to be true, our minds will require to make room for the new fact. Many things, long considered incredible, are true. In our voyage in search of truth, facts are the infallible stars.

When we read the New Testament, we find a number of men and women trying to make room in their minds for a new fact. Jesus has appeared in the world. There are many mysterious things about His birth and life and death and resurrection, but most mysterious of all is Jesus Himself. We express the mystery by saying, 'He is the Son of God'. In His own time, people found it easier to convey the same thought by telling of the wonderful things which He did. We call them 'miracles'.

What is a miracle? 1. We might say, 'It is something which science cannot explain.' A hundred years ago, if a man in Edinburgh had seen something happening at that moment in London, he would have declared, 'This is a miracle!' Yet to-day we do not speak of television as miraculous. We might put it this way, that things go on being 'miracles' for centuries, and then suddenly cease to be 'miracles'. It might be better, then, to alter our definition and to say, 'A miracle is something which science cannot *yet* explain.' Even to-day science does not know everything. (It is quite possible, for example, that the nucleus of an atom is 'as complex and as thickly populated as the city of London'. There may be a whole world of activity of which we know nothing.) It is certain that there are many facts waiting to be discovered. For all of them our minds will have to make room. Many of them we are probably trying to explain now in ways just as quaint as that of the Arab who was asked what the telegraph was, and replied, 'Suppose that you have a very long, thin dog, so long that its head is in Damascus and its tail here in Beirut. When you pull its tail here in Beirut, the dog squeals in Damascus. That is the telegraph.'

2. Since science has much still to discover, it might be better to say, 'A miracle is something which is contrary to the laws of nature.' We are not now using purely negative evidence, which may be upset by the discovery of a single new fact, but positive evidence, which has a mass of facts to support it. We are able to tell superstitious people that spilling salt does *not* bring bad luck. The idea that it does will not *fit in* with what we know already about God and His love. In the same way, it might be said that the laws of nature are there, whether science has discovered them or not, and that the laws of nature cannot contradict one another. And that would be true.

But it would not be the whole truth. If it were, we might go on to say, 'A man cannot walk on water.' That would be falling into the mistake of saying 'Impossible!' and then, perhaps, discovering some new power which explained everything quite simply. But there is something even more important to notice. Whenever we speak of 'a man' we are dealing with that which is not controlled by the 'laws of nature'. Lord Kelvin said, 'Every action of free-will is a miracle to physical, chemical, and mathematical science.' We may say, quite accurately, that every movement we make alters the world of nature. When an engine strikes the wagon at the end of a goods-train, the bump goes from wagon to wagon, right to the end of the row. It may be very slight when it reaches the last wagon, but it is never reduced to nothing, however long the train may be. Move your hand, ever so slightly, and the whole of the earth's atmosphere is disturbed. The whole world of nature has to readjust itself.

> All things by immortal power,
> Near or far,
> Hiddenly
> To each other linkèd are,
> That thou canst not stir a flower
> Without troubling of a star.

Though the readjustment may be infinitesimal, we may not disregard it. Among the Alps, a single shout has been known to set free an avalanche. A tiny readjustment may have profound consequences.

We have spoken of things which science cannot *yet* explain. Here, in human wills, we have that which science can *never* explain.

Science has done very much to trace the course of evolution, but the fact of life, of intelligence, of the rise of organic creatures from an inorganic world, of the appearance of man in the animal kingdom—these are all beyond the power of science to explain. This reminds us that we may frequently be forced to *fit in* facts, without being able to explain them. It is the facts which alone can give the explanation of the rest.

3. But we are now reminded of the existence of a

science of the human mind. Our definition might be altered, therefore, to read, 'A miracle, if it is authentic, is something which implies powers, hitherto unknown, in the human personality.' The extent of this realm has also been considerably reduced in our time, for, in the facts of telepathy and the powers which the mind is found to possess for the cure of bodily illnesses, we see things which we should no longer wish to describe as 'miraculous'.

4. Thus we turn our attention away from that which, in all probability, will some day be explained by the science of the human mind, and direct it to something which *can never be explained* in terms of human personality. This is what we call a 'miracle' when we are speaking from the side of religion and the Christian faith. Just as the laws of nature are independent of our discovery of them, so the activity of God is there, whether or not our human personalities co-operate with it. When we say 'miracle', we mean that God is at work. And by that we do not mean simply that God is working in the familiar ways, sustaining the universe and inspiring human personalities. We mean that He is at work in special ways. We might call it God's free-will. Just as, when we ourselves act, we change the course of nature, without, however, breaking any of the laws of nature, so God intervenes for higher ends—it may be for the relief of suffering, for the advancement of goodness, for the salvation of men—and He does so without making nature contradict itself. What we find at work is a law, *within* nature, which is *higher* than nature. And this, as might be expected, is observed most in real crises of history and in response to conspicuous faith.

Belief in miracles is simply our confession that God can do new things.

Why did Jesus do miracles? We read of times when He refused. The story of the Temptation in the wilderness shows that Jesus would not consider the possibility of using His power to do what we might call 'conjuring-tricks'. He would not perform wonders simply in order to prove His power. Belief, if it had been forced in that way, would not have been worthy belief. Nor were His miracles intended as signs to establish the truth of His teaching. We are not to think of them as a kind of bugle sounded by a man to call attention to his message. If the miracles had been intended as signs of the power of God, and nothing more, they would have appeared where faith was lowest. On the contrary, they were part of the message itself. He performed the miracles in order to reveal what God was like. Here was a case in which the human personality was not weak nor erring; instead, it co-operated perfectly, and in all things, with the activity of God. In the miracles of Jesus, therefore, we see the *true* order of things breaking in. We begin to realize that the obstacles and troubles of the world were not meant to be. Jesus set Himself to remove them. The only con-dition was that men should co-operate with Him. That is what we mean when we say that miracles are granted only in response to men's faith. Men can always have the old, bad order if they desire it or if they do not believe in any other, but God wants them to have the new, divine order.

Did Jesus need to perform the miracles? I think we must acknowledge the possibility that some of the stories in the Gospels are misunderstandings or misinterpretations of what actually took place. Jesus was above His reporters. It is very probable that some of the miracle-stories were originally parables, which have been mistaken for actual events; others were the reflection of prophecies in the Old Testament; others, again, spiritual experiences of the disciples. But many of them are clearly the straight-forward account of what Jesus did when He was con-fronted with trouble or sickness among men and women. He always takes it for granted that disease is part of the

H

kingdom of evil, and He sets Himself to remove it. 'Jesus, in fact, seems to have felt towards physical and mental disease precisely as every good modern physician feels towards it.' In answer to our question, Did He need to perform miracles? we say: He could not help performing them: He loved mankind so well.

Running through all that has gone before is the answer to the other question, *How did He work miracles?* The answer is that His perfect life on the earth revealed the Divine, the true supernatural; not only God's Power and Love, but also God's Liberty to help men and women in whatever need He found them.

Can we still expect the performance of miracles in our own day? We may answer that question first with a caution. We cannot expect the followers of Jesus to do what He did. They have not His faith in God, nor His power of imparting faith to those who are in need. But we must answer it, secondly, with an affirmation. Healing miracles, in the sense of works which cannot be explained in terms of human personality alone, are by no means uncommon. The conquest of many forms of bodily and mental disease has been made possible only through the courage and devotion of Christian doctors and surgeons, often at the cost of their lives. We read, for example, of a missionary doctor in China. His people are dying of a strange plague. Deliberately, one day, he goes into the laboratory and swallows some of the germs. The progress of the disease will be carefully watched, and, even though he should lose his own life, his action will save the lives of thousands of his people. In sacrifice we are confronted with that which is more than human.

Unfortunately we live in a time when faith in God is not the warm and living thing which it was in the days of the New Testament. We do not expect great things from God, and the result is that we do not receive what would otherwise come our way. To the blind men whose eyes

He opened, Jesus said, 'According to your faith be it unto you.' Our age may not be an age of great faith, but ours is not to be taken as the standard for all time.

When men become more like Christ they will have a greater share of the powers of Christ.

EDGAR P. DICKIE

Can you Prove that the Story of the Resurrection is True?

'CAN we prove that the Story of the Resurrection is true?' Well, if you want what is called pure scientific truth, we cannot. And there is great gain in saying so at once. But let us hasten to add that the whole purpose of the Resurrection was to convince us of a spiritual Truth: and spiritual truths are not scientifically demonstrable. Spiritual Truths are matters of Faith: Pure Science oversteps its bounds when it exceeds a summation of facts. But if, by the question, you mean you are 'worried about the Resurrection', perhaps we can help.

Most folks who are worried about the Resurrection have done a bit of reading. They have read that 'these things happened' in a very credulous age, when miracle was commonly accepted. They have read, too, that Christianity, in claiming that its central figure rose from the dead, is only claiming what many pagan religions had already claimed for their particular Gods. They, therefore, assume at once that the Resurrection of Jesus Christ was just another of these. To put it bluntly, they think it was a hoax spread abroad as a legend to suit the purpose of the early Church. Now the trouble with these 'scientifically minded' young people, who swallow that explanation, is that they fail rather lamentably to be scientific. If they are going to dabble in this comparison between Christianity and other religions—that is, explore the science of Comparative Religions—they must obey the first rule of any science, which is to consider *all* the facts. And if you explore all the facts, you find there is no real parallel at all. Certainly there were ancient religions of the East that claimed that their God had risen from the dead; but if you examine them you will find that they were always, so to speak, putting the claim farther and farther back. It was always 'thousands of years ago' that it happened. But this is not true at all of Christianity. We can date, as a scientific fact, when Jesus lived on earth, and we can date, as a scientific fact, when His Church was growing by leaps and bounds—inspired in its splendid faith solely by a conviction of the Resurrection. And the time that elapsed between His death and the commencement of His Church is so short that it precludes absolutely the possibility that the vitality of the Church in the first century was based on a 'hoax legend'.

You try to get together a secret society to-day, and spread the hoax that you have seen a dead man rise out of a grave. If you all kept the secret and spread it sedulously it *might* happen that in perhaps a hundred years folks would believe what once you had invented. But could you for a moment suggest that you would get folk to believe it within sixty days? Yet it was in something like that time that the Church was being founded, solely on a belief in the Resurrection! Indeed, we can go farther. Could you get folk to believe it, in so short a time, if in the beginning you were not inclined to believe it *yourself*?

Here again, if we are to be scientific, we must sedulously take account of all the facts. If the Scripture record worries you, you must at least be careful to take account of all that Scripture says. And Scripture tells us that even the followers of our Lord were not expecting the Resurrection early on Easter morning. 'When they heard He was alive and had been seen of Mary,' says the Marcan record, 'they disbelieved.' The Gospel of Luke is even stronger and says of the first report of the Resurrection: '. . . these words appeared in their sight as idle talk.'

Whatever else we can make of this, at least it proves to us that credulous as was the age, they were not ashamed —in this regard—to record their incredulity: at least

these words would not have been likely to be put into the
record had the inner circle of the very early Church in
fact been endeavouring to create a legend!

Indeed, this scientific line of approach to the Gospel
story leads us to a further consideration. It is astonishing
the number of people who tell you they cannot accept the
Resurrection story, and when probed for their reason, at
once reveal that 'what they cannot accept' are aspects of
the story which the Gospels at least have never asked
men to accept! They come out with such statements as
'I can't believe that Jesus was seen as an ordinary man
walking about on Easter morning. . . . I cannot believe
every one saw Him'. Now, nowhere in the Gospel story
is it claimed that every one saw Him: nor do they claim
that He was seen as an ordinary man. There were, in fact,
only three recorded occasions on Easter Day when He
was seen: and each record has some element of mystery.
He was seen of Mary . . . but at first she took Him for the
gardener, and spoke to Him as to a gardener, till He revealed His full personality . . . even then He said: 'Touch
Me not.' Again, when first He appeared to the disciples,
who were together in a room, the door being shut, 'they
were affrighted, supposing they beheld a Spirit'. Most
significant of all, He walked and talked with the two
disciples on the road to Emmaus for several miles without
their recognizing that He it was who accompanied them.
True the Gospel record makes it clear that He was more
than a Spirit, He said so to the disciples; and at the end
of the journey to Emmaus, He broke bread with them.
But His appearances were not ordinary. They were,
what the Church has always claimed, something unique.

And indeed, for men of faith, it is only along this line
that the Resurrection story reveals its true significance.
All the Church has ever claimed is what emerges clearly
in the Gospels—namely, that He appeared only to those

who in some sense were waiting for Him and seeking to do His Will. It was to Mary, who was *seeking* Him, that He vouchsafed His presence. The disciples, before His Death, He had told 'to keep together'. And it was only when they had *the courage to keep together*—and it needed courage—that He revealed Himself on Easter evening. There is no record that Jesus revealed Himself to any of the disciples while they still 'dismissed the tale as idle talk'! And on the road to Emmaus 'their eyes were holden that they did not know Him' until it was towards evening, and they asked the Stranger to accept their hospitality and to spend the night. *When they stopped asking questions, that is, and did the Christian thing* . . behold, He was made known to them in the breaking of bread.

Certainly these are not proofs 'that the story of the Resurrection is true'. But is there not at least emerging a very different Resurrection story than the rather fictitious one that so many minds create for themselves, and then get worried because they cannot believe it? The ultimate proof of the truth of the Resurrection comes only to those who humbly accept the possibility of such appearances as have been recorded.

But there is a final, scientific, and most important aid to faith. It is unscientific to rest the whole case on the Gospel story, and the inductive approach from the experience of the centuries is of profound significance. Many of the so-called 'proved facts of science' to-day rest entirely on what are called inductive theories, because men are dealing with the kind of fact that is not capable of complete proof. If, in some realm of science (runs the inductive method), a sufficiently large number of experiments all point unerringly to one assumption: that assumption becomes for the scientist 'the fact' on which he works until he can find a better one. And an inductive proof of the Resurrection is simply that an unlimited number of 'experiments in living' have been made, through the Christian centuries, based on the assumption that Jesus Christ rose from the dead. And every one of these experiments, when truly made, has so far pointed unerringly to the truth of the assumption.

Whenever men 'ask' honestly, as the disciples were asking on the road to Emmaus, and add to their inquiry the grace of Christian charity—He is given to them. Whenever folk seek, as Mary sought, He is found of them. Whenever men knock, as the disciples were knocking on the door of truth as they assembled on Easter evening, the door is opened to them. The universal experience of faithful men unerringly points to the truth of the assumption.

The assumption is, of course, Pure Shining Miracle— That it was God who 'begat us again to a lively hope by the Resurrection of Jesus Christ from the dead'. Nor do any who have found Him require to explore any other assumption: for there is no better one than that.

GEORGE F. MACLEOD

What do You mean by the 'Fall' of Man?

EVERYBODY who does any serious thinking at all must have been puzzled from time to time by the problem of human beings. What are we to make of this race to which we belong—so like other animals, and yet so very different?

There are moments when we think of Man as a superb and dazzling creature—the inventor who conquers earth, sea, and air, and explores infinity with his microscope and telescope; the genius who builds cathedrals, composes symphonies, creates poems and dramas; the happy warrior who is daunted by nothing and is willing to sacrifice his life for another or an ideal. 'What a piece of work is man!' says Hamlet. 'How noble in reason! How infinite in faculty! . . . in action how like an angel! In apprehension how like a god!'

Then there are other moments when we feel quite disgusted and ashamed of the whole race. We see Man smashing the fairest things he has built, quarrelling, thieving, being monstrously cruel, jealous, and vindictive. And we remember, perhaps, how Gulliver told the giant about the habits of the human race and received the verdict: 'I cannot but conclude the bulk of your natives to be the most pernicious race of odious little vermin that nature ever suffered to crawl upon the surface of the earth.'

So it is natural that the various religions and philosophies have adopted different theories about Man. You can roughly group them into the optimistic and the pessimistic. The optimistic theory is that of the man who looks at the chess-board and says: 'It's white—with a few black squares.' The pessimistic theory is that of the man who says: 'No; it's black—with a few white squares.' In other words, some have been convinced that human nature is fundamentally good; and others that it is hopelessly evil.

The Christian doctrine of the Fall of Man is an attempt to summarize what the Bible has to tell us about Man's nature. I would call it neither optimistic nor pessimistic, but realist. Roughly, it is that Man is created by God and for God, and therefore has a capacity for goodness, truth, and beauty far beyond any other created thing we know; but this capacity has been distorted and deflected by evil. Man is made to become a 'son of God'—that is, a creature who is able to reflect God's love, purity, joy, and creative power: but he is a Prodigal Son, a son who has got lost. In other words, Man is neither totally good, nor totally bad, nor yet just a random mixture of both. He is a glorious being gone wrong, a good thing spoiled.

The doctrine of the Fall, then, is a Christian description of the sort of people we are. It is based on what the Bible has to say, and it corresponds to what we can observe for ourselves. It doesn't attempt to account for the disaster that has occurred, to tell just how, and why, and when Man went wrong. The story of Adam and Eve and their expulsion from the Garden of Eden is not an historical account of how the Fall happened. It is a description, in poetic form, of a present fact. We *are* fallen creatures—and the story of Adam and Eve is the story of you and me. *We* give way to temptation, *we* try to become gods ourselves, *we* go wrong and then try to blame someone else. And we do so because we are fallen creatures.

Sometimes people who dislike this doctrine try to blame the Apostle Paul for its introduction. Well, he gave a pretty clear picture of this nature of ours, but we don't have to go beyond the Gospels to find its essence. You will have noticed how Jesus always

treated men and women as if they were what we call
V.I.P.s. They were of infinite value in his eyes. And
yet he was quite clear about the sin, the radical sin, in
human nature. 'If ye then, *being evil . . .*' he said once,
not addressing vicious people or his special enemies,
but ordinary friendly folk. He was never deceived or
shocked by what people did, 'for he knew what was in
man'.

The doctrine of the Fall is not a grim and gloomy
doctrine as is often imagined. It contains within it a
great promise for humanity. For to be fallen is not a
hopeless condition: it suggests at least the possibility
of getting up again. Let me take an illustration. Suppose I look over the edge of a dirty stream and see
among all the slimy creatures that live there a little dog
struggling in the mud. I immediately guess that it has
fallen over the edge and try to lift it out. I don't bother
to take out the other creatures: it's their element and
they belong there. The dog does not belong there. He
has fallen. Do you see what I mean? When we say
Man has fallen, we mean he doesn't belong to the evil
in which he lives. We don't give him up. We believe
in what the Bible calls his redemption, his deliverance.

So it comes about that Christian people who have
grasped this doctrine are not so easily upset by the grim
events of to-day as are those who have taken a lighter
view of human sin. The strange thing is that the very
people who now take a hopeless view of human nature
and say they have lost faith in it altogether are often the
same people who thirty years ago scorned the Christian
doctrine of sin, and proclaimed that man was infallibly
on the road upwards. Those who begin with the theory
that sin is only a passing phase, something we can be
educated out of, are the ones who end by despairing of
the human race altogether. The Christian knows that

Man is fallen, but believes that through the grace of God he can be lifted up again. Once we admit that Man is lost (that is, has lost his way) we can hear the message of the one who came 'to seek and to save that which was lost'.

D. H. C. READ

In What Way is Christ my Saviour?
The Redemption

IT is not easy to answer shortly the question, What is
the Redemption? You know how many answers can
be given to another question which is often asked and
discussed: Why did we join in the Great War? Some will
say, because we were bound in honour to do so; others
that we were fighting for democracy or freedom, and
others again that we were forced into it to save our own
existence or our own interests. Now scarcely any of these
answers are altogether false; in fact they help each other
out, the probable truth being that our motives were complicated. One no doubt dominated, but it does not tell
the whole story. Similarly with the Redemption. It is so
rich in love and wisdom that a simple explanation won't
suffice. There are people who sneer at it and call the story
childish or unworthy of God, and it is best not to listen to
them, because they have not tried to understand it. If I
try to explain it by story or parable, remember that they
are only to serve as clues.

In the Bible our Lord is called the Lamb of God who
takes away the sins of the world, and the prophet Isaias
saw the Son of God carrying our sorrows and wounded
for our iniquities. We had gone astray and the Lord laid
on Him the wickedness of us all. Suppose that a gang of
bandits in the United States were caught and brought to
justice. They had taken many for a ride, smashed up
families, kidnapped children, and shot down many inno-
cent persons. Their brutality, it was felt, must receive its
deserts, and even if one of the judges were the father of a
man in the gang, he would feel forced to put aside the
feelings of a father in order to administer justice. In other
words, unless such blackguards as these are punished, we

should feel that something was wrong with the world and with justice. Next, let us suppose that the President of the United States has a son who is the finest type of man and at the time engaged on a work of national importance with a picked body of companions. An appeal is made by the gang from the verdict to the President and his son comes to hear of it. He straightway obtains an interview with the criminals and he says to them. 'Look here, I don't believe that you are absolutely rotten and I will do my very best to help you. I can take you on under me in the work I do, which is very hard and important, on condition that you swear to give up entirely the life you have been living and suggest yourselves some punishment which will show the world your regrets for the past and your good intentions. I am prepared to trust you to the extent of going guarantee for your good behaviour and I will persuade my father to agree to this.'

The son was an irresistible pleader and won his way with his father, and at first the gang, thinking they had got off on very easy terms and were now in for a soft job, played up. But they all hated hard work, and their leaders, the sort that would have murdered their mothers for a dollar, soon persuaded the rest to put the blame for every inconvenience on the son. One day they turned on him and smashed him up and then made off with him. They reckoned on using him as a ransom and so saving their skins. I will not go on with the story, as it has served its purpose. There is a parable in the New Testament like to it of the householder and the husbandmen. The gang are all mankind, and if this seems exaggerated, remember that people like ourselves put Christ to death, that we human beings have made the world the unhappy place it is, and that the poverty around us, the immorality, the wars between classes and between nations are our work. If such evil sickens us what must it appear to the Author of all good, in the light of His perfect purity and before

His justice. God would not be God if He did not show His abomination of evil and vindicate His justice, and it is this justice which appears first in the Redemption. The marvel is in the way that God who is also love so works that justice and love kiss. Love brings the very Son of God to be a man with men, one of us, who can appeal to our love and also be our one boast before the justice seat of God. He identifies Himself with man, and now a man can say to God, 'Behold a true human son who loves you as you would be loved and begs in return a love from you for all mankind, his brothers.' As in the story, He is our guarantee; He is prepared to make atonement. And what an atonement! Instead of being grateful we hated Him and hung Him up upon a tree. One might think that love had failed and that now justice would follow with punishment and doom. But out of the very worst of evil springs a marvellous good, and the justice finds its victim in the sufferings of that Son of Man, who beseeches God that His pain may be taken as sufficient sacrifice for the sins of those who slew Him and the whole of mankind. Such inimitable love is irresistible. Justice is satisfied; the greatest act of affection that has ever been offered to God and to us is combined in that willing sacrifice of Christ. He is now the Lamb who takes away the sins of the world. Being lifted up to die on a gibbet He draws all to Himself, and as St. Paul says in a magnificent image, He blotted out the handwriting of the sentence of our condemnation, nailing it to the cross in His own flesh.

Here is part of the secret of the Redemption. There is more in it than this, for He so identified Himself with us by love that what He suffered we ought to have suffered and what He became in the Resurrection we actually become, heirs of Christ and co-heirs, the sons of God, flushed, so to speak, though we feel it not, with His risen glory and His divine strength, vine branches of the vine of God, 'that the love wherewith thou hast loved me.

may be in them and I in them'. This is almost too sublime to speak of, and reaches out to the mysterious truth of the Mystical Body of His Church and the Holy Eucharist. But I hope that you see how God had to be just and how by a wondrous stratagem He combined this justice with love; that this was done by the Son of God becoming man, acting in our name and turning the rejection of himself by us into a sacrifice of infinite power to God for us. 'By his bruises we are healed.' God suffers the penalty of evil done and pours out upon us the love due to the self-sacrifice of the one guiltless man who was also God.

M. C. D'ARCY, S. J.

What is 'The Holy Spirit'?

NINETY-NINE men out of a hundred take their 'colour', as we say, from their surroundings. Put them in a merry company, and they will be merry; bring them into a sober environment, and they will be sober; let them mix with drunkards, thieves, and vagabonds, and they will be exceptional indeed if they do not sink into a career of vice. It is true of men, as of God (though in a very different sense), that with the merciful they show themselves merciful; with an upright man, upright; with the pure, they are pure; and with the froward, they learn frowardness.[1] Whenever two people associate together, each catches something of the spirit of the other. And where one is strong of character, and the other weak, the weaker will inevitably fall into the ways, the habits, the vices, and even, though less easily, the virtues, of the stronger.

God is incomparably stronger than man. And, therefore, if man 'associates' with God, he will infallibly fall in with God's ways; his character will in some slight measure become like God's. He may help this process forward by disciplined effort of his own; but, however weak and poor his effort may be, so long as he is willing to be dominated by God, the change will come about in him by something akin to the psychological process of which we have been speaking—a process set up whenever two characters are associated together, and most of all when one is strong and the other weak. This is what the Bible calls 'receiving the Holy Spirit', or 'the Spirit of the Lord', or the 'Spirit of Christ'. The natural question to ask, therefore, is: 'What do you mean by "associating with God"?' But, before we consider that, let us inquire a little further what the New Testament has to tell us about this 'receiving the Spirit'.

[1] Cf. Psalm xviii. 25, 26. See A.V. and Prayer Book version.

I suggest two great texts for you to consider. The first asserts that the Holy Spirit is like *the wind*: 'The wind bloweth where it listeth, and thou hearest the sound thereof, but canst not tell whence it cometh, and whither it goeth: so is every one that is born of the Spirit.'[1] We all know that characteristic of the wind—its overwhelming power, its freedom from control, its refusal to allow itself to be mastered, bound, or fettered. Many people in consequence have thought that in this text 'receiving the Spirit' means becoming irresponsible, undisciplined, eccentric, and arbitrary; and many spectacular religious movements have suffered terribly, and done untold harm, because they have fastened on this idea, and made it their watchword, to the exclusion of all others. But it is wrong to take a single text and make everything depend upon it. The Bible cannot be treated like that with safety. And another text will help us to correct this first impression.

The second text is constituted by a single phrase, 'Walk in the Spirit'.[2] Nothing is less like the violent fury of the wind than the plodding perseverance of the walker; it speaks to us of the virtues of decent citizenship, not of the eccentricities of wayward genius. And St. Paul means what he says. A few lines later on he tells us what 'walking in the Spirit' is really like: its fruit, he says, is 'love, joy, peace, longsuffering, kindness, goodness, faith, meekness, temperance'[3]—all very sedate and orderly qualities, but none the commoner for that. It is only when we put these two texts together that we reach the true secret of the way in which the Holy Spirit works.

For it is not so easy as it sounds to 'walk in the Spirit'. When we are faced with the temptations, difficulties, disappointments, and disasters of ordinary human life, the virtues which St. Paul calls 'the fruit of the Spirit' seem suddenly all to disappear, and we become hard, selfish, mean, unfriendly, and morose. Indeed, we can only

[1] John iii. 8.   [2] Gal. v. 16.   [3] Gal. v. 22.

'walk in the Spirit' properly if the Spirit of God is blowing in upon our hearts like the gale of which the first text speaks, or burning there like fire. For God is love; the first 'fruit' of the Spirit is 'love' as well—just as 'the more excellent way' in which the Spirit comes is by giving us a love for God, for our fellow men and for righteousness, which 'suffereth long, and is kind; envieth not, vaunteth not itself, doth not behave itself unseemly, seeketh not its own, is not easily provoked, thinketh no evil, rejoiceth not in iniquity, but rejoiceth in the truth; beareth all things, believeth all things, hopeth all things, endureth all things'.[1] What is it that helps the ordinary husband and wife to make a success of marriage, in spite of all the drudgery, anxiety, and troubles that it brings? Just a love of this sort for one another and for their children. What is it that enables the Christian to overcome temptation, and prove himself helpful to his generation, his Church, his family, and his neighbours? The same love expressed more fully towards God, and towards the world at large.

By associating with God, we have said, we begin to partake of His Spirit; that is, to show a love like His. But how do I 'associate with God'? Briefly enough, by trying to learn more about Jesus—to do the things that are according to His will—to pray that the purposes which He cherishes may be brought to full effect—by living in close contact and intimate communion with all who are trying to serve Him faithfully. That is how we associate with God, through Christ, in the Church; and those who attempt to maintain such an association need never fear that they will be left helpless in the face of the many overwhelming responsibilities that are laid upon them. For the love of God will be shed abroad in their hearts by the Holy Spirit which is given them;[2] and love is the strongest of all forces known to man.

KENNETH OXON:

[1] 1 Cor. xii. 31; xiii. 4-7.   [2] Rom. v. 5.

What is the Soul?

TO start with, soul means just life. The familiar initials 'S O S' stand for 'Save our souls', and this means 'Save our lives'.

The Animal Soul. Now, there are many kinds of life. Plants, for instance, have life, though it sounds fanciful to talk of them as having souls. So far as we know they do not feel or think, but they act: they absorb food, they grow and multiply, they decay and die. Animals have a larger life. At the lowest levels it is hard to distinguish between plant and animal; but there is no doubt about the difference when we mount higher on the scale. Even the most splendid oak shows no sign of feeling or perceiving. It is different with animals. It is indeed hard to say what their life is like, for they have no words with which to tell us. But at least we may be certain that they feel pleasure and pain, perceive the things about them, have many impulses similar to our own, and that the higher animals show the rudiments of thinking. With these marks of life it does not seem fanciful to speak of the animal soul.

The Human Soul. In these respects the soul of man is like the animal soul, but it differs from it in many ways.

In the first place, the human soul has an idea of itself. Man knows himself as continuing the same being throughout the changes in his body and the growth of his mind and character. It is memory that makes this knowledge possible, and the memory required is not merely the recurrence of some experience that has occurred before. Sensations, perceptions of things, feelings, impulses, acts, occur; and others similar to them afterwards recur. But I have memory only when the new experience is recognized as having occurred before in my own life. One continuing life or soul is needed in order that there may be memory, just as, on the other hand, memory is needed to make us aware of our continuing life. What sort of memory is shared by animals we cannot tell. But it must be narrow in range, and is probably different in kind from man's.

In the second place, the soul has not only an idea of itself and its body. It forms ideas of the things surrounding it in space and time, discovers their relations, and forms science; it has ideas of other selves (or body-souls) like itself and of their grouping in family, nation, and race, and begins to understand history; it discovers rules or principles which may serve to guide it in choosing between good and evil in action; and it learns to produce things which will satisfy it not only by their usefulness but by their beauty. Science and history and philosophy are among the greatest achievements of the human soul, or of what (because intellect is so prominent in them) we should rather call the human mind.

At the least, therefore, we must say that the soul of man is of a higher order than the animal soul.

Body and Soul. Man is body-soul or body-mind. We may call him animate body or embodied soul. In what way body and soul are united in one being is a question of great difficulty. There are many theories about it, but no general agreement among those who have most closely studied the subject; and it cannot be discussed here. Nor will I discuss the evidence produced by the Society for Psychical Research, partly because it is not generally accepted by men of science, partly because it is not confirmed in my own experience. Leaving this out of account and restricting ourselves to normal experience, some statements may be made with confidence:

1. Certain changes in the body lead to changes in the soul or to its disappearance altogether; certain changes in the soul lead to changes in the body, but never to its complete disappearance. This is a fundamental point of

difference, and due weight must be given to it. It shows that our lives are dependent upon their material embodiment in a way in which the material embodiment is not dependent upon our lives: but it does not show that soul is a mere 'function' of matter organized in a certain way. We knew before that life and, still more, mind are late and rare visitors to the material realm, and their origin is unknown. But they do not enter matter from the outside: they animate it and leave it. As no man now alive has ever been dead, there is no one to tell us what death means to the soul.

2. As we pass to higher levels of mind it becomes increasingly difficult to connect a particular mental event with a particular bodily event. If we ask: What event in the brain corresponds to my conviction that I, who am now thinking, am the same self as thought on the same subject yesterday? no physiologist can answer. The same may be said about the reasoning of the mathematician or the metaphysician, and, indeed, of many simpler matters.

3. If we are tracing the organization of matter and what happens at each stage, we are inclined to look upon mental activity as a function of brain. But if we are thinking of our own life and its purposes, then we look upon brain as the instrument of mind. Both views may be justified, if one is not taken to exclude the other.

4. In any case, soul and its activities are entirely unlike matter and its movements. For instance, there is no resemblance at all between the pain of toothache and decay in a tooth with its resultant neural disturbance. Closely as they are connected, soul and body belong to different orders of existence.

Soul and the World. The poet Keats called the world a 'vale of soul making', and the phrase has gained currency in recent years. It is in the world that a man discovers and makes his own soul. For his soul does not remain unchanged, but is formed by the life he leads. Sometimes it may be allowed to revert almost to the animal level, and then it is easiest to regard it as just a function of the body. Or it may aim at higher things, for attaining which the body is, at best, merely an instrument. A writer with a deep knowledge of human nature gave a list of such things in this piece of advice: 'Whatsoever things are true, whatsoever things are honest, whatsoever things are just, whatsoever things are pure, whatsoever things are lovely, whatsoever things are of good report; if there be any virtue and if there be any praise, think on these things.' Many men do think on these things and strive to reach them; and, in so doing, they are beginning to raise their souls not indeed out of the world, but above the world.

Thus the soul of man is not the world's creature only; it is also the world's interpreter and in some ways its master. It comes to understand the laws of nature, seeks to unravel their meaning by the help of ideals which nature itself did not supply, and makes an effort to bring the world into greater harmony with these ideals. The spirit of man (for here the term spirit may be preferred to soul) need not disdain its humble beginnings, for it is able to link itself with things that are eternal.

W. R. SORLEY

Do you Believe in the Resurrection of the Body?

THE Resurrection of the body cannot be understood unless we first understand what the body is. The body is a material thing, but it differs from other material things in being alive. Life means a relation to personality, what we sometimes call a soul, or 'I myself'.

The body connects the person with the material world, and that in two ways. Firstly, the body is the person's instrument by which he works upon the material world; and, secondly, through his body a person may be affected, injured, punished, coerced, either by the hand of nature or by those of other men. It is, for example, because we have bodies that we, though immaterial persons, can be shut up in prison or beaten or tortured. The body is thus the means through which immaterial persons suffer. It is also in itself, by its imperfections, and by its liability to disease, the source of much that is humiliating and painful to the person to whom it belongs. All diseases are unpleasant, and many of them degrading, and some of them revolting. And the curious change which we call growing old happens to every one, and, though taken for granted because it is universal, is yet distressing. All this seems irreconcilable with the goodness and the omnipotence of God.

We who believe in a good God cannot believe that the body as it now is fulfils His ultimate purpose. It is clearly a failure as it stands. God must intend something better than this. Some would solve the problem by supposing that after this life men will have no bodies. Most of those who think thus seem to believe that there will be no further connexion between the material world and human beings who have passed through death.

Christians indeed believe that there will be an intermediate state after death and before the Resurrection of the body, though its character is unknown. But it seems impossible to believe that God tried the body and placed mankind in the material world as a kind of experiment which has failed; and that because of its failure He is going to throw it on the scrap-heap, like an unskilful mechanic. We must think that God intends to make something of the material world and of mankind in relation to it, and that therefore some such device as a body, which brings persons into relation to matter, must be part of His permanent purpose. We can believe anything more easily about God than that He should ultimately fail.

Let us now hear what Holy Scripture has to say. St. Paul in two places very impressively teaches the Resurrection of the body.[1] This he does by two figures of speech. By one he compares the risen body to some fruit springing out of a seed and much more perfect than that seed. By the other he compares the risen body to a house prepared in heaven with which we shall be one day clothed. We must beware of taking figures of speech too literally. We are not dealing with a precise definition of some chemical process or mechanical device. But St. Paul's general meaning is perfectly clear. He means that the risen body, though a body, is yet to be something much better and finer and more perfect than the natural body we now have. It is to be what he calls a spiritual body, a body that is more completely under the influence of the human immaterial spirit, and not like our present bodies, imperfect and the means of our suffering and servitude.

Then we have a glimpse of the risen body of our Lord. If you read the last chapters of the Gospels according to St. Luke and St. John you will find that Christ's body is represented as having been drawn up again out of the

[1] 1 Cor. xv and 2 Cor. v.

tomb by His personality, leaving the tomb empty and the grave-clothes lying where they were. The careful account by St. John of the position of the grave-clothes is clearly meant to emphasize this. Christ has resumed his power of bodiness (if I may use that old-fashioned word). He is able again to use matter as an instrument and to express Himself through matter. But there is a very marked change. Matter is now altogether His servant. He can change His appearance at will. He walks with two friends to Emmaus, a distance of about seven miles, and talks to them expounding the Scriptures, and they do not recognize Him, until at the last He assumes His accustomed face and form and then vanishes out of their sight. Again we read that He appears to the Apostles twice in an upper chamber with the doors closed; and that there He invites the touch of St. Thomas's hands and is willing to eat before them. And He always appears clothed, as it seems, which means of course that He has used matter to make Himself clothed.

All this shows a new relation between personality and matter. Christ can do what He likes with matter; it is absolutely subject to Him. He raises the old natural body from the tomb, but we may guess that that was for other reasons than necessity. He wished to give a sign that the Apostles could understand; and He wished to save the matter, which had been consecrated by union with Himself as His body, from the dishonour of putrefaction. These may be our conjectures; but at least it is certain that when the body was raised it was absolutely subject to Him, so that He could change it and use it as He pleased. Here we see illustrated St. Paul's teaching of a spiritual body, a better, more perfect body, more entirely under the control of personality. St. Paul indeed speaks of Christ as the first-fruits of the Resurrection. His is the example of the risen body and of what the Resurrection of the body really means. St. Paul, looking forward to the coming of Christ, says that we shall not all die, but that we shall all be changed. This is the same thought—that the relation between personality and matter will be different. The spiritual body will supersede the natural body. Now we are what we are, subject to disease and pain and senile decay, limited also by all the laws of matter, so that we must conform at every turn to the system of the material world. But the spiritual body is to be absolutely subject to us, and to emancipate us from, not to enslave us to, the dominion of matter.

St. Paul also looks forward to a profound change in the material world. For there is in the material world the same inconsistency with the goodness of God that there is so notably in our own bodies. St. Paul foresees that Christ will complete His work, and that as He has already redeemed personality—the soul—He will redeem the body; and not the body only but the whole material creation.[1] But this is too large a subject to discuss now.

When I say, then, that I believe in the Resurrection of the body, I mean that there will be restored to us the power of bodiness, that is the power of expressing ourselves in matter; and we shall again have bodies to be our instruments. These will be much more perfect instruments and will correspond much more exactly to the character of our personalities; nor shall we be subject to any of the laws of matter or through them to pain or restraint. But our bodies will still be real bodies, which can be touched and seen, like the body in which Christ appeared after His Resurrection. There is no need to think that they will have any material connexion with our present bodies, though I suppose personality could use afresh the same atoms if they were available. Christ had doubtless His own reasons for saving the matter of His natural body, which would not apply to us. But we shall be masters of matter in virtue of the restored relation

[1] Rom. viii (best in Revised Version).

of bodiness, and able to express ourselves as we may choose. And we shall be fully redeemed in mind and will, so that what we choose will be according to the will of God.

QUICKSWOOD

Do we Really Know Anything at all about Life after Death?

I DO not pretend to be able to say anything new or startling. I can only try to state what I believe Christianity has to say on the subject, guided by the light of such new truth as the Holy Spirit has been revealing to this generation. For it is good that we should be reminded that knowledge can never be static, and it is exceedingly unfortunate that the text 'the faith once delivered to the saints' is often used as if it meant that the Holy Spirit had finished His work of revelation. He is to lead us into all the truth, and truth is not only many-sided, but often mysterious—in its ancient sense, something hidden but ready to be revealed. I am not going to deal in any way with the debatable question of being able to communicate with those who have passed over, because Christianity says little tangible about it, and though some well-known and greatly respected scientists believe in it and its value whole-heartedly, they know it has great dangers which will make ordinary folk leave it alone, unless they do it from a scientific standpoint. It is also to be noted that some people who treat it as a religion definitely attack not only the Churches, but the great truths of Christianity itself.

I want to say at the outset that the Christian idea of the Resurrection is much more than mere survival; the Greeks and Latins practised clairvoyance and had ideas of a future life. But the Resurrection of Jesus Christ was a new factor in history, a definite revelation of God's Power which brought hope and joy to mankind; and it was the preaching of this which changed the world.

Now, though we know little on the whole about the future life, Christianity has a real message about it, and we can find great comfort from that message, as well as real warning. First of all, a man may ask what evidence we have for survival. The answer, surely, is that if you believe in Christianity at all you must believe in a future life, or the Life, Death, and Resurrection of Jesus Christ have no meaning. God is love. He calls us His children, and loves us while here, and it is inconceivable that death should bring all his loved ones to an end. Moreover, Jesus said to His disciples, 'I go to prepare a place for you', and more striking still, to the thief on the cross, 'To-day shalt thou be with me in Paradise.' 'Thou . . . with me'—two personalities together in the future life; our Lord knew where He was going and that He would not be alone. That 'to-day', too, helps us to realize that we start that new life straight away and do not sleep for ages waiting for a resurrection, as people used to think, and some hymns seem to suggest. It has been truly said that 'death is but a bend in the road of life'. Death is the gateway to a new life, not to age-long sleep, and though our bodies may be laid in a grave, we ourselves—our personalities—enter a new kind of life. One of the reasons why I hope when I die that my body will be cremated is because sometimes relatives and friends, and especially children, who are too often allowed to go to the grave-side, are apt to think that those who are buried are actually in the grave; they go like Mary and Martha to weep at the grave, but do not see Jesus standing outside and saying, 'He that believeth on Me shall never die.' My body may be ashes—our bodies will all come to dust —but I, we, our personalities will enter into a new life.

But again, a man may ask: 'But what shall we be like? Shall we just be disembodied souls, whatever that may be?' And it seems to me that the answer is given by St. Paul when he says, 'There is a natural body and there is a spiritual body.' The natural body we know, the spiritual we cannot describe. Our Lord, according to St.

Mark, the earliest Gospel, says 'they are as angels in Heaven' when refuting the Sadducees' question about the Resurrection, expressing a truth in picture language which they could understand. After the Resurrection our Lord Himself appears with a spiritual body, which makes one believe that the body has a form similar to our present body, by which recognition is possible. Of course, it is a mystery which will one day be revealed, but some instinct within us surely tells us that there will be recognition in the fuller life so that we may know those we have loved here and renew our fellowship there. Do we not also picture the future life as a home, a fellowship, a communion? A state, that is, where love reigns and we shall have objects to love just as we have communion now with those who have passed over.

Is it not because love is eternal, and fellowship through God, who is Love, so real, that the veil between this world and the next is so very thin?

May I give you a personal experience? Last year, when my sister was just about to follow her twin sister to the future life, and be united again with her who had passed on only the year before, I felt an almost overwhelming desire to ask her to give my love to her twin, and it certainly did not seem in any way incongruous; perhaps she was there with us in the room—I don't know; but I am sure the veil is very thin at times between this world and the next. But this I do know, her true personality is as real to me to-day as it was when she was here.

Again, the question will be asked: does Christianity suggest what we shall do in the future life? I imagine we all have ideas about this, and I hope we have got over making material what has been given us in picture, symbol, or poetry, such as playing on golden harps, or singing in the celestial choir, or sitting by streams in the Elysian fields for ever and ever; for these pictures are enough to make the future life appear a thoroughly boring existence. Here a parable may help us; our Lord certainly seems to suggest in the Parable of the Talents that the reward for service here will be further service in the life beyond. Our Lord, we are told in St. Peter's Epistle, went to preach to the spirits in prison, and as Love is service we can only imagine that we shall have the fulfilment of Love by opportunities of service in the life beyond. Rest as portrayed in the future life, it seems to me, can only be taken in the sense of that line in one of our hymns, 'In perfect work shall be perfect rest'.

Again, Christianity implies that there must be growth in our characters in the life beyond. Although our aim here is perfection, no one is perfect when death's call comes, and I cannot see that the process of death is going to make any difference to our personalities; we shall pass over just as we are. 'To be with Christ, which is far better', St. Paul says, that is our hope and will be our joy, so that we may be transformed into His image from glory to glory. But as we are not perfect when we pass over, and perfection is God's purpose for us, it is clear that there must be growth; and that as we are given a perfect perception of what God's love and purpose is we shall grow into the stature of the fullness of Christ.

Again, some one will ask, What about the question of punishments and rewards of which we read so much in the New Testament, and, indeed, in our Lord's words? There can be little doubt that Christianity teaches that this life is a preparation for the next; and however much we may revolt—and rightly, I think—against the material pictures describing hell, there can be little doubt that Christianity speaks of a future judgement for all and especially those who have deliberately refused to live according to the light that has been given them. We are told that our Lord Himself, who knows what is in man, his difficulties and his trials, will be the Judge who is merciful and of great kindness. And I doubt if all the pictures of a material hell-fire would be as bad as looking into those eyes of Love when we have deliberately rejected Him and the highest that is in us, and we realize that He knows the flimsiness of our excuses. It is true that some of us make our own hell here and we may be passing through its purifying fire now, but it is not all the truth. If there were no future life in which men would come face to face, perhaps for the first time, with the knowledge of the despicable cruelty, inhumanity, and utter fiendishness of their treatment of God's children, Love itself would not be true to its nature, there would be no possibility either of reformation or redemption, and some would say, retribution.

Once more, Christianity teaches that in the future life we shall be able to comprehend the Beauty, the Wonder, and the Love of God Himself; now we know only in part, but then shall we know even as we are known. At present our vision is often so feeble, the mystery of God's love is only partially revealed, but to be with Christ, to see God dealing with His children as Christ did, to find the explanation of all those things we find so difficult to understand now, and to know Him who is all Love and Beauty, Goodness and Truth, that is surely worth striving for and making our aim now?

May I then sum up what I have been trying to say? I have dealt, I know, only with part of the subject and only from the Christian standpoint, which needs, and can only be apprehended by, what is called faith, that step which we all must take beyond what is called reason if we are to achieve the Christian life, the step which God calls us to take as little children of a Heavenly Father. This is what it seems to me to say, that through the Resurrection of Jesus Christ from the dead, Death is not the end of *us*, though it is of our natural body; that it is the entrance for us, our personality, to a new and fuller life with a spiritual body through which recognition will

K

be possible of those we love in the Family of God; that we enter that life with the same character and personality with which we leave this; that we shall not remain static, but be given a chance to grow towards perfection; that as we have tried to be faithful here to what is highest, God will give us further service in the life to come, and there in the blessed fellowship of God's children the Father will reveal Himself to us, and we shall know what Love really means.

For this is life eternal, that we may know God and see Him face to face, without sin and without shame, through His everlasting Love and Mercy.

And is there not a message in all this for you and me? May I suggest two things.

First, the thought of the future life should keep us young in mind; this life is so small a proportion of life as a whole, it will make us continually eager to learn to be ready for fresh wonder, as we approach the gateway to this new life.

Secondly, it should brace us to new effort. We do not want to go to that life shrivelled and useless personalities who have learned nothing but self-gratification, but strong, virile, living souls who have done our bit to work out the eternal purpose of God through serving our generation with His help. God knows we have made mistakes, and often failed miserably, but if this has been our motive and we have shown the Christ-like spirit in our relation to others in reliance on Him day by day, He will see amongst all the dross something of the image of Himself, and it will enable Him at the last to make us grow into His likeness, into the measure of the stature of the fullness of Christ.

PAT MC CORMICK

Is there no 'Eternal Life' for Good People who Lived before Christ?

THIS is the poser that has been put to me. But can I answer it? If I am asked to shoot a stag, I may reasonably claim that I must get to some spot where I can clearly see my quarry, respectfully pointing out that I cannot shoot through trees or round sharp corners. Similarly, I must be quite sure that I can see this question clearly before I can hope to answer it. I am not acquainted with my questioner, and therefore I must analyse his question in order to be sure what it is he wants to know—if, indeed, I can tell him; for I take it he wants to know, he does not want merely my opinion. Is a perfectly clear Yes or No possible to this question?

My questioner has learnt from the Bible that for those who are in Christ, or believe in Christ, there is eternal life. By 'eternal life' he understands, I suppose, not merely some kind, any kind, of future life but a blessed future life, life, as the Bible puts it, in the 'Kingdom of God' or, simply, heaven. I am asked whether those who lived before Christ, even if they were good, faithful, god-fearing men, are excluded from heaven or this eternal life; is heaven for Christians and for Christians only? To this question happily there is a direct answer in the Gospels. In St. Matthew viii. 11 and 12 I read, 'I tell you, many will come from the east and west and sit at table with Abraham, Isaac and Jacob in the kingdom of heaven, while the sons of the kingdom will be thrown into outer darkness.' I do not fully understand that, but at least it is quite clear that 'eternal life' in the teaching of Jesus Christ is for saints of the Old Testament as well as for those who believe in Jesus Christ while they are on earth.

Or did Abraham, and Isaac and Jacob really believe in Jesus Christ, although He was not yet come? That is too deep a question for me; yet we ought to look at it. In Mansfield College chapel in Oxford there is a remarkable series of stained-glass windows representing the saints of the Christian Church throughout the ages, but in a corner of the chapel is a small double window of which one panel depicts Amos representing Prophecy and the other depicts Plato representing Philosophy. Is it proper, decent, Christian, to put up a stained-glass window to the Greek philosopher, Plato, in a Christian church?

In the old traditional creed of the early Christian Church in the West, which gathers up the teaching of the apostles, we read that Jesus Christ 'was crucified, dead and buried; He descended into hell; the third day He rose again from the dead.' Our translation, 'He descended into hell', is misleading. Not the place of punishment is meant, but the place where, as men believed, the dead waited for the day of Judgement. For three days, we might say, Christ joined those who are in the grave. There is a strange passage in 1 Peter iii. 19, which says that Christ 'went and preached to the spirits in prison'. This does not prove anything, but it points to the belief of the early Christians that those who had died before Christ came had a chance of hearing His Word and therefore of responding to it.

This belief, then, we may say, is in the Bible and the creed, but we must put it in different terms to-day, if we are to understand it. I suspect that the thought of many has been held up in this matter by a genuine if misguided idea of what is involved in loyalty to Christ. It is by Christ we are saved—through faith, and Scripture tells us that there is no other name given under heaven whereby we must be saved. It would seem to follow, therefore, that only Christian believers can be saved; perhaps by a kind of concession it has been thought that the patriarchs and prophets and saints of the Old Testament might be included also in the number of the saved; but once it is suggested that Plato or Virgil or Confucius or the Buddha might be saved, we seem to be denying that salvation is by Christ and Christ alone. We seem, then, to be on the horns of a dilemma: either we are saved by Christ alone, in which case there can be no eternal life apart from personal belief in Christ, or else there is eternal life for Plato and other good non-Christians, and in that case it is not Christ who is the only Saviour. But we are not really shut up to those alternatives.

A boy at school was asked by his master, 'What is electricity?' After a long pause, he replied, 'I did know once, but I am afraid I have forgotten!' Upon this the master said, 'Here is one of the great tragedies of human history! At last someone has arisen who knows what electricity is—and he has forgotten!' It is possible to *use* electricity without having any idea what electricity *is*. In the same way it is not difficult to think that men might be saved by Christ without ever knowing who He is; indeed, up to a point that is plainly to be seen. For instance, our hospitals and our social services really spring from our Christian tradition; we owe them to the teaching and the inspiration of Christ; those who have never really heard of Him, and who certainly are not Christians, are saved from much suffering and misery by Christ. How far could we extend that principle? Could a man have 'eternal life' because of Christ, if he had never heard of Him? That sounds unreal, but there are two theological ideas to be here considered.

First, in the New Testament Jesus Christ is called the Word of God. 'In the beginning was the Word . . . all things were made by Him . . . and the Word was made flesh and dwelt amongst us.' What is meant by 'the Word' here? It is the eternal purpose or plan of God, or better, it is God in His eternal purpose towards the world. God has a purpose in Creation; He has revealed that purpose in many ways and many fragments to prophets, poets, and saints throughout the ages; through them He has spoken to the heart of man; His Word to man is Christ; He revealed something of Christ to Moses, to Jeremiah, to Plato, to Confucius. But in Jesus Christ, the Word made flesh, He perfectly revealed His Purpose. If we look at things in this way, as did some of the early Christian teachers, we can see that the prophets and saints and poets and teachers of mankind have in some degree really believed in the Word of God, though they never heard of Jesus. It is not really nonsense to speak of the prophets as Christians before Christ, for it was really in Christ they believed, though He had not yet come in the flesh.

Second, the Bible gives no support to the view that the soul of man is intrinsically immortal, that God is so kind that He will provide eternal life for everybody anyhow, that we are saved, therefore, not in any real sense by Christ, but by the general, universal kindness of God. It is to Christ alone that the Bible ascribes salvation. But there are important and well-known passages which indicate that the coming of Christ affects more than the few who have believed in Him. 'We have believed', for instance, 'that this is the Christ, the Saviour of the world'; 'Behold the Lamb of God that taketh away the sins of the world.' We ought not to water this down to mean that Christ is potentially the Saviour of the world but not actually, that He would like to take away the sins of the world, but can only do it in a few cases. Christ, the Son of God, took our human nature upon Him. The Bible conceives the whole human race as one 'in Adam', bound together in our common sinful rebellion against God. It conceives that God Himself in Jesus Christ identified Himself with us—with humanity as a whole. It is as if into a diseased body there is inserted at one point a healing remedy which will gradually spread and cleanse and heal the whole. The purposes of God are not fulfilled during Man's short time on earth. Only in Christ is there salvation and eternal life, but Christ is related to all men, not only to those who have heard His name and responded to Him. To my question, therefore, 'Is there no "eternal life" for good people who lived before Christ?' I should answer that there is eternal life for all who here or hereafter, in this world or the next, open their hearts to the grace of God made known to us in Jesus Christ our Lord.

NATHANIEL MICKLEM

Is there Such a Place as Hell?

THE Bible often speaks of Hell as if it were a place to which the wicked go after death. One of the words used is the name of a place outside Jerusalem, where refuse used to be burnt. We also read of a 'lake of fire' into which the Devil is to be cast. Other words used for Hell in the Bible simply mean the place to which people go after they die. Sometimes the wicked are said to be in torment after death. It is very difficult for us to imagine what life will be like after the death of the body. In any case, it is clear that it will in many ways be very different from the life which we now live on earth. So when the Bible describes Heaven and Hell as though they were 'places' it seems best to take these descriptions as parables setting forth the truth about the other world in picture form to help our understanding. It would certainly be a great mistake to take them quite literally.

The important question for us to decide is not whether Hell is a place, but whether the teaching of the Bible about Hell is true. In other words, will there be Final Punishment for the wicked?

The Gospels tell us that God is our Father and that He loves us perfectly. He is 'kind toward the unthankful and evil'. Yet our Lord's parables also speak of God's wrath against sinners. Can the same God be both a kind father and also a stern judge? Think of the best kind of human father. He knows the difference between loving a child and spoiling him. If we are allowed to have our own way always, we shall probably become thoroughly selfish. So a father shows a higher sort of love when he is ready to correct or even punish his son for wrong-doing. Such a father wins the respect and love of even a difficult boy, if the stern treatment has deep love behind it. All this must be true about God in a much higher way, since He is perfectly wise and holy as well as loving.

The story of the prodigal son tells how a sinner may repent and be welcomed home by his heavenly Father. But let us suppose a different ending to the story. Let us suppose that the son had remained in his wicked ways in the far country. Then he would have been cut off from the home by his own choice, living in loneliness and misery. This is a true picture of what sin can do to any one of us if we turn our backs upon God's love. It can actually banish us from God's presence, and that is the worst thing that could happen to us. Those who have happy homes and kind parents can imagine how terrible it would be to be banished from all that happiness through their own fault ; for example, if they were justly sentenced to a long term of imprisonment for committing a serious crime. Sin can banish a soul from God's presence. This must be so because Holy Love and Sin cannot dwell together. If a selfish man were to go to Heaven, he would not enjoy it. The unrepentant sinner could not enjoy living with God.

We are told that when Judas Iscariot hanged himself 'he went to his own place'.[1] Wherever that 'place' may be, it could not be God's place. For, unlike the genuine repentance of St. Peter, the remorse of Judas was merely selfish and despairing. So it could not make him fit for God's presence. His sad story tells us how sinners make their own Hell. For Hell is where God cannot enter; and if any man refuses to let God enter into his heart, that man is surely making Hell for himself. He has wandered into the far country and is feeding himself upon husks. His punishment is simply to have what he has chosen, and if that choice becomes fixed and final, then the punishment must become eternal. There is nothing arbitrary about God's ways with us. His love

[1] Acts i. 25.

towards the sinner does not change. It remains always the same, however much we may provoke Him by our wilfulness. God does not want to punish anybody. His desire to save us from our sins is so great that He gave His Son to die for us upon the Cross. Yet we can refuse the gift which He holds out to us. We can turn our backs upon the way to Heaven if we wish to do so.

At this point, however, it is quite natural to feel a serious difficulty. If any one is really doomed to suffer eternal punishment, it would seem to follow that in such a case God has been finally defeated. If one single soul is lost God's Love has failed to win that soul to repentance. There seems to be no way of avoiding this conclusion. Perhaps we may be inclined to say: 'If God is almighty, why can He not abolish Hell altogether and by His almighty power bring everybody to Heaven at the last?' To this question, at least, the answer is clear. God could not do such a thing without destroying the power of free will which He Himself has given to us. When God gave to each of us the power to choose between right and wrong, He knew well the risk involved. He knew that any of us might prefer evil to good. Yet He thought it worth while to give us this power, because without it we should be no better than the animals. Indeed, if God had made us so that we could not help being good, we should have been like 'robots' or like mechanical toys which are wound up and have to do what their maker meant them to do. As it is we have the power, if we choose, to ruin our lives. But we also have the power, by God's help, so to live that we may become like God and enjoy His love for ever. Surely this makes all the risk and difficulty worth while! God will not force any one to do right. He leaves us free to choose, because that is the only way in which we can really become good. It is the only way in which we can learn to love God, as He should be loved by His children.

There is only one way to Heaven, the way of repentance, which means forsaking all sin and giving ourselves to God with all our hearts. This we must do for ourselves with the help of that grace which God gives to all who ask for it. This is *our* responsibility. *We* must choose. Will there, then, be any who do *not* choose sooner or later to give their hearts to God? We do not know. There is a great deal which we cannot know in this life about these deep matters. It may be that in the mercy of God, some time and somehow, all sinners will of their own free choice repent. Then God's love will have won the final victory over evil. But we cannot say that it must be so. Again, if any refuse the offer of God's love to the last, it may be that they will be destroyed by their own wickedness, so that they will no longer exist. We cannot tell. If it should be so, it will not be for any lack of love on God's part. For He loves to the end. In any case we can be sure that if any sinner *does* go on resisting God's love to the bitter end, that sinner will be a lost soul. This is a terrible thought. But for those who have learnt to know God's love it is a good thing that they should face this terrible truth for their souls' health. Our Lord said: 'Fear him which is able to destroy both soul and body in hell.' And St. Paul wrote: 'Work out your own salvation with fear and trembling; for it is God which worketh in you both to will and to work for his good pleasure.'

In conclusion we may be sure that God will deal with us according to the use which we have made of the opportunities which have been offered to us. The heathen man or the child of the criminal underworld, who have never heard the Gospel, will not be expected to have lived according to Christian standards. We cannot set limits to the patience and forbearance of God in dealing with His children. On the other hand, we who have received God's gracious invitation must not presume upon His goodwill. 'God is not mocked: for whatsoever a man soweth, that shall he also reap.' If I resist God's love I cannot look forward to the future with either confidence or hope.

L. S. THORNTON

Is it Possible to Reconcile the Thought of Eternal Punishment with an All-Loving God?

THE first point is that all those descriptions of hell and its physical tortures, which have been dwelt upon in many sermons and by many writers, are not Scriptural at all. We have inherited them from Milton and Dante and other writers, and from painters. All this account of the tortures of the damned, the physical tortures of the damned, you will not find in Holy Scripture at all.

That is the first point. Then you go on a little farther, and you say: 'Well, what does Holy Scripture teach us?' It teaches us three things. It teaches the doctrine of eternal punishment. Eternal punishment is spoken of again and again in Holy Scripture, and, if you come to think of it, so long as the sin is eternal, the punishment must be eternal too. In one place we pray to be delivered from eternal sin. A great writer says, 'When self-will ceases hell ceases.' All through, Scripture distinctly lays down that there is such a thing as eternal punishment; it does not say how many will inherit it. But the awful thing about which our Lord warns us was that the will might be so bent the wrong way that it would not be able to turn at all.

The second point is that Holy Scripture nowhere reveals what that punishment is.

Thirdly, everywhere Holy Scripture reveals that, whatever it is, it will be consistent with the Love of God.

Then come three other points which I think will help us very much. We notice that hell is compared in the New Testament to Gehenna. Now what was Gehenna? Gehenna was the fire outside Jerusalem which burnt up the offal and refuse of the city, which were cast upon it.

There were three things about Gehenna; it was placed outside the holy city; it was placed where the offal and refuse were burnt; it was not outside the government of the Roman Empire. In these three points hell is like Gehenna. It is outside the holy city; secondly, it is a place where the morally infectious are kept from harming others; but, thirdly, it is not outside the government of the just and loving God. In other words, God is the God of hell as well as the God of heaven. And that makes all the difference. We have been erecting in our minds two gods, one called the devil, and the other called God. This is impossible! God is love behind hell as well as behind heaven, and therefore we must get out of what is really the old Manichaean heresy of imagining there are two gods, one the devil and the other God. God, who shows such wonderful power, is the God of hell as well as the God of heaven; and just as Gehenna was not outside the government of the Roman Empire, though outside the holy city, so hell is not outside the government of God. Therefore the thing to hold on to is this, that God is not justice to some and love to others, but that God is justice and love to everybody; hell is not like Norfolk Island in the old days, where criminals were turned loose to look after themselves. Those who are in hell, whatever hell is, are still under the government and under the care of God. As Bishop Bickersteth says so beautifully in one of his books: 'There is room for the display towards even the crushed and humble ones of that everlasting mercy which is the emerald rainbow around the throne of God.'

A. F. LONDON

'Lead us not into Temptation'—but Would God Lead us into Temptation?

THE Lord's Prayer hardly began to be used in the Church before this very difficulty was felt. More than sixteen centuries ago Christians were using paraphrases of the petition such as these: 'Do not allow us to be led into temptation', or 'Lead us not into temptation greater than we can bear', or (a combination of the two) 'Do not allow us to be led into temptation greater than we can bear'. Here we have two chief ways of meeting the difficulty. One says that God may allow temptation without actually causing it: the other suggests that temptation is not an evil unless we succumb to it, that temptation overcome may be a valuable discipline. I think that one or both of these solutions would still be tried by many in tackling the problem to-day.

We can approach the question in three ways. (1) We can ask what exactly the petition meant for Jesus. (2) We can ask what may be learned from the life of Jesus to illustrate the petition, remembering that the life of our Lord is the best commentary on the Lord's Prayer. (3) We can look at our own experience and try to understand the petition as applied to the temptations that actually come to us.

1. *The meaning of the petition.* It is found in Matthew vi. 13 and Luke xi. 4. The wording (in Greek) is identical in the two places. There are two questions here: (*a*) the meaning of the verb 'lead'; (*b*) the meaning of the noun 'temptation'.

(*a*) The verb is used in the Greek translation of the Old Testament to render a Hebrew verb which means literally 'to cause to enter'. Most commonly the object of the verb is a thing, and the verb then means 'to bring into'. The natural meaning of the verb in the Lord's Prayer would accordingly be 'Bring us not into temptation', and this is the translation given in the Revised Version. But it is possible for the Hebrew verb which means 'cause to enter' to have the slightly different meaning 'allow to enter'. So the petition *might* mean 'Do not allow us to enter into temptation'. But though it is possible, I do not think it likely.

(*b*) The word 'temptation' can be understood in two ways. We may think of all the inclinations which we have towards wrongdoing; and this is the way in which most people understand the word. Or we may ask what the word meant at the time when the Lord's Prayer was given to the disciples. Among the Jews of that age 'temptation' had acquired a special meaning in connexion with religious persecution. It had come to stand for the 'trials' which a loyal Jew might have to suffer for his faith: it is the same thing as 'persecution for righteousness' sake'. This kind of temptation was apt to be the fiercest of all, and those who succumbed to it fell into what was in Jewish eyes a most deadly sin—the sin of apostasy. I think that the word means something like that in the Prayer. We ask that we may not be brought into such straits that the only way of escape is by denying our religion.

2. *The example of Jesus.* Here we must take account specially of two Gospel narratives. One, the Temptation Story,[1] is placed at the beginning of the public career of Jesus: the other, the Agony in the Garden,[2] almost at the end. Our Lord was not only not immune from temptation: He had to face it throughout His ministry. And it is at its fiercest at the end. It is of the essence of the matter that His temptations are always shown to us as temptations to abandon His ministry in favour of

[1] Matt. iv. 1–11; Mark i. 12, 13; Luke iv. 1–13.
[2] Matt. xxvi. 36–46; Mark xiv. 32–42; Luke xxii. 40–6.

something else. By leaving His task He may achieve what men desire: staying at His post He must face the extremity of suffering. In Gethsemane He is face to face with this terrible choice. The only thing that can deliver Him from it is some act of God. The prayer of Jesus in the Garden[1] is surely our petition from the Lord's Prayer applied to the situation as it is at the end of the ministry. We may note these points: (a) Temptation is a terrible reality for Jesus; (b) He believes that God *can* deliver Him from it; (c) He does not hesitate to ask God to deliver Him from it; (d) He submits Himself entirely to the will of God. Christians must not seek an immunity from temptation which Christ Himself did not have: they must seek rather to face inevitable trial with His faith in God and His willing submission to God's will.

3. *Our own experience* at least confirms the first of the four points just mentioned. Temptation, in every sense of the word, is a reality, a terrible and inescapable reality. The experience of temptation is part and parcel of human life on earth; and if 'Lead us not into temptation' means 'Let us not be tempted at all', it is asking for the moon. We are already in temptation, just as we are exposed to disease, accidents, and lots of other painful experiences. The question 'Why does God allow us to be tempted?' is only part of the much larger question, 'Why does God allow evil at all?' We may well be perplexed about the presence of many strange things in the world—temptation among them. But we shall not solve the problem by denying their existence. The only answer to the question 'Would God lead us into temptation?' is that, whoever is responsible, we *are in temptation* constantly.

Now this thing that we call temptation, what is it? A rough and ready description, which should, I think, cover all cases, would be that it is the conflict inside us between what we believe to be the will of God on one

---

[1] Mark xiv. 36.

side and the pull of evil forces on the other. That conflict is going on in every human life. What can the Lord's Prayer mean in the light of that fact? Consider what happened in Gethsemane. Jesus says: 'Remove this cup from me', and 'Not what I will, but what thou wilt'.

The first thing to note is the faith of Jesus that God *can* 'remove this cup', that is, deliver Him from the impending and terrible test. And He does not hesitate to ask for that deliverance. That means that Jesus felt all our natural human shrinking from pain and suffering. It means that we need not hesitate to say in our prayers what we really want. A great deal of time is wasted in asking God for things we think we ought to want: it is one of the subtlest forms of hypocrisy. It is as natural for us to dread all the various kinds of 'temptation' as it was for Christ to dread the supreme 'temptation' of the Cross. We should feel as free as He did to tell God of our fears and shrinkings and to ask Him to deliver us in any given case. In the particular case, when we are faced by something that is going to test our courage, honesty, patience, loyalty to friends, ultimately loyalty to God, the general petition 'Lead us not into temptation' becomes 'Remove this cup from me'.

But along with this cry for help goes the other equally definite cry of loyalty and devotion, 'Not what I will, but what thou wilt'. Though we dread the ordeal, we must recognize that God's will comes first. Therefore, along with the simple, frank expression of our natural desire there goes the act of complete submission to the will of God. It comes to this, that we say to God: 'Save me from having to face this ordeal; but if I must face it, then give me strength to come through it undisgraced.'

It can be immediately objected that this explanation is not really logical. We are presented with a dilemma. If temptation is a bad thing we are quite right to pray for deliverance from it, and God ought not to lead us into it.

More than that, He cannot lead us into evil, so that ultimately the petition is superfluous. If, on the other hand, temptation is according to the will of God, then we ought not to seek to be delivered from it. The answer to that is threefold. First, the Universe, as we know it, is not so cut and dried as all that. We cannot pretend to know all about it and all about its Creator. We grope our way and still do most of our walking by faith and not by sight. Secondly, human nature—thank God!—is not purely rational. We are a queer mixture of hopes and fears, strength and weakness, reason and emotion and primitive instinct. Thirdly, Jesus Himself somehow could hold together in one prayer the cry for deliverance and the assertion of absolute loyalty: He could at once shrink from and yet accept the trial.

To sum up: when we use this petition we must use it with the meaning that it has for us in the light of Christ's temptations and our own experience. We must be able to say to our Father in Heaven, 'Lead us not into temptation', and mean by that *both* 'Remove this cup from me' *and* 'Not what I will, but what thou wilt'. Thus the petition becomes an acknowledgement both of our weakness in the face of trial and our ignorance in face of the mystery of the world. And in acknowledging our weakness and ignorance we cast ourselves completely on the power and the wisdom of God. When I say to God, 'Lead me not into temptation', I am speaking—I confess—not as one severely rational being to another: I am speaking as a child to my Father and I am acutely aware of my weakness and ignorance and content to rely upon His strength and wisdom.

T. W. MANSON

Why does God make Sin so easy and Goodness so difficult?

I ALWAYS distrust (don't you?) the person who can't answer a question without asking what the question means. On the other hand, if I am asked a question, I find that I always do it myself. This time, I think there is really some excuse for it. The question, as it has reached me, doesn't quite explain which of two things it means.

Suppose somebody tells you, 'Well, I think I've at last succeeded in making my dog enjoy his dinner!' You would immediately ask, 'How did you do that? Did you alter the dinner, or did you alter the dog?' He may mean, you see, that he has gone on experimenting with different kinds of biscuits until at last he has found a brand which has secured the dog's approval. Or he may mean that he has conditioned the dog—by starving it, by beating it, by running round after it and shoving a plate under its nose—to like the kind of dog biscuit which *he* thinks good for it. Two quite different things; and there is the same kind of confusion about the question we are discussing here. 'God makes sin easy'—in what sense? In the sense that he has chosen to label sin all sorts of things which you and I rather enjoy doing? Or in the sense that he has made you and me the kind of person who rather enjoys doing certain things which, regrettably enough, are sinful?

As a matter of fact I think sin is a very boring subject, and I would rather take the other half of the question if you don't mind; it will all come to the same thing. 'Why does God make it so difficult to be good?' It is a good thing to get up and let an old lady have your seat in the train. But it is not a comfortable thing to do; the corridor is anything but comfortable. Now, what is the complaint exactly? Are we complaining that God should have labelled kindness to old ladies GOOD instead of BAD? Or are we complaining that he has made us the kind of people who don't enjoy standing in a corridor?

First, then, let us put the question like this: 'Why has God labelled so many uncomfortable things GOOD?' And the answer to that, of course, is that GOOD and BAD aren't mere labels which God attaches arbitrarily to this or that, like the railway people labelling one carriage 'Smoking' and another 'Non-smoking'. God didn't sit down and *arrange* that certain things should be good and other things bad. We are not to think of him as trying to make up his mind (if I may put it like that) whether to write down on tables of stone, 'Thou shalt not honour thy father or thy mother', and then deciding, in the end, that it would look better the other way. No, goodness is not something which God invents; it is Something which God *is*.

That is an idea, of course, which makes one's head spin. But you have got to face it if you are going to talk sense about God at all. Goodness is his nature, and he cannot be false to his own nature; his Almightiness stops short of that. How can I offer any illustration of the idea? Well, imagine a very good artist, who is called upon to say what he thinks about a particular picture; is it a good picture? And he sees at once that the thing is a daub. Well, he may want to spare the feelings of the person who asked him—a relation, perhaps, of the artist. But he *cannot* say that it is a good picture; he has to shuffle and get out of it somehow. He *cannot*; he has a tongue in his head, which would form the syllables, yes; and on any other subject he wouldn't, perhaps, be frightfully particular about telling the truth—he would lie unblushingly to a Customs officer. But on that particular subject he *cannot* bring himself to tell a lie; his artistic sense, which is a great part of his personality, forbids it.

Do you see what I mean? In that *sort* of way God cannot love what is evil; he cannot approve of you or me doing something wrong. For that wrong thing is not simply something which he has decided to *call* wrong; it would be a denial of, a treachery to, that human goodness which is the reflection of his own nature. Goodness is something which he cannot help loving, for that reason. The unselfishness which makes you get up and stand in the corridor, although the old lady is no relation of yours, and nothing to look at, and probably you will never meet her again, is something he cannot help loving. After all, it is an infinitely distant, infinitely pale reflection of Jesus Christ hanging on the Cross. If he didn't love what is good he would stop being God; that is the point.

I hope I have said enough to make it clear that *in one sense* the question I am trying to answer is meaningless. God didn't make man, and then study his habits, find out what he enjoyed doing, and tell him, out of mere spite, that it was his duty to do the opposite. No, we have no grievance against him for telling us to do the kind of things we don't enjoy doing. If we have any grievance against him, it must be for making us the kind of people who don't enjoy doing things like that. We have no grievance against him for telling us to obey our fathers and mothers. But why didn't he make us the kind of people who enjoy obeying their fathers and mothers? In that second sense, the question still remains to be answered. Couldn't God have made us in such a way that it would have come natural to us to be good?

At first sight, that is an easy one. The answer is that

that is exactly what he did; he made us in such a way
that it came natural to us to be good. Only something
went wrong on us—the Fall. It doesn't matter, for our
present purposes, how literally you take the story in the
third chapter of Genesis, or how metaphorically; the
point is that, the Christian tradition tells us, we were
built for a destiny which we have missed. Everything
else in creation lives by the law of its own being; Man
alone is a misfit. To do, all the time, things you don't
approve of yourself for doing; to be, all the time, something you wish you weren't—what destiny could be
more ludicrous? You might as well be a carnivorous
rabbit. Man is a fallen creature; the freewill he enjoys,
which was meant to be a kind of parachute that would
enable him to float among the clouds, has turned inside
out, and is no better than an umbrella to keep the rain
off him here and there. . . . A fallen creature.

Obviously we could go on and on about that. But
it would be silly to ignore the come-back which
immediately occurs to all of us—granted that there
were human beings, centuries ago, to whom it came
natural to be good, what use is that to you and me?
We aren't like that; and what have we done, that we
should be born into a world in which, admittedly, we
are misfits? God doesn't make carnivorous rabbits;
why does he make human beings who tell lies although
they know it is wrong? We know, of course, that when
our Lord Jesus Christ came to earth, he brought with
him a solution of the difficulty—grace. We know that,
somehow, grace restores us men to the position we had
lost; we are once more God's children. But, grace or
no grace, we still find the same old trouble. Sinful
things attract us; doing the right thing comes to us,
usually, as an effort, and an unwelcome effort. Is it
fair that we should be made like that?

I think we'd better avoid that word 'fair'. It implies

the question, 'By what right has God made me what I am?', and that, obviously, is going to be a difficult philosophical point, which will make us look fools if we are not careful. No, the question is, 'Why?'; and you answer that question, not by considering whether the thing is fair, but by considering whether the thing is reasonable. Is it reasonable that you and I should be condemned to this amphibious kind of existence, in which we feel like fish out of water all the time, continually disappointing ourselves by not running to schedule, by not living up to the heights of our ambition? Even so, it's a difficult sort of problem to tackle. And I suggest that the right way to go about it is to ask, 'Does this state of things fit in with the conditions under which I am living here and now? Is it in line with all the rest of my experience of the world?' If it does, then I think we are at liberty to describe it as 'reasonable'.

And surely it does. We have lost our Paradise, and we are born into a world-order which is, if you like, a kind of second-best, but it is the world-order we are accustomed to. We are conditioned, you and I, to a world of struggle, in which nothing seems really worth having unless it has taken something out of you to get it; in which nothing seems really worth doing unless you put something into it. Even the beasts around us survive and maintain themselves by activity. ('A certain amount of fleas is good for a dog; keeps him from thinking about being a dog.') Struggle is the condition of obtaining even the material things which keep us alive; a few people here and there get legacies or win football pools, but by long and large we only get what we earn, and we have to work if we would earn it. And if that is true where our material welfare is concerned, it is still more obviously true in things of the spirit. Our amusements—what is the fun of a game which doesn't cost you some effort, either of brain or of muscle? The creative arts—who ever produced a masterpiece without going through agonies of mind in the production of it? Falling in love—is it possible to be really in love when you are only thinking what you can *get* out of it, instead of being constantly anxious to *give* something?

I suggest, then, that under our present conditions of living there is no value without struggle. All the ardours and splendours of life are mixed up with doing things that are hard to do. And wouldn't it be all wrong if religion, which is so obviously meant to be the most splendid thing in life, had, under our present conditions, no difficulty attached to it? If we kept the commandments as effortlessly, as instinctively, as we eat buttered toast, should we have any respect for the commandments, or for the people who kept them? Oh, no doubt it's only a sort of second-best, this mortal life in which we serve God so badly, and so reluctantly. But isn't it rather a glorious kind of second-best, being left to work out (under God's grace) our own destinies? We cheered to the echo when Mr. Churchill as Prime Minister said he had 'nothing but blood and sweat and tears' to offer us; might we not expect the same offer from the Crucified? Mayn't we even feel, in a curious way, rather honoured to have been entrusted by our Captain with the post of liaison, half-way between the angel and the beast? It would not be a post of honour, if it were not a post of striving. In this world of fallen nature, striving has become a kind of second nature to us. We are like the fishes that keep their heads up stream.

I applaud the question I have been trying to answer. It is not the idle, captious question of a heckler who wants to make trouble; it raises a deep philosophical problem. The problem, I mean, how what is good fails to exercise an irresistible attraction over us; or, to speak more accurately, how we find ourselves more attracted by something not-so-good than by something better. And the answer seems to be that we live in a topsy-turvy world, or the thing couldn't happen. Somehow, the Fall seems to have reversed the gear of our nature, and we live, now, under conditions in which a thing has got to be difficult if it is going to be worth while. So it would be foolish of us to doubt that doing the right thing, instead of the wrong thing, is worth while. Because God knows it is difficult.

R. A. KNOX

Why is it wrong to do Wrong?

THE question is a puzzling one because it is so very simple and searching. I think the thought behind it is something like this: 'There are a lot of things which we are supposed not to do or which we are forbidden to do or which we are punished for doing, because they are said to be wrong. What makes them wrong? Who says they are wrong? If I like doing such things, if I get pleasure out of them, if it pays me to do them, why shouldn't I?' And these are questions which we all at some time or other ought to ask ourselves and to which we must find some answer, because they concern fundamental choices in the way we live our lives and because the lives of others, of our neighbours and our children, will in a great measure depend on the answer we find and the choice we make. Why shouldn't I push my ball into a more convenient place if my opponent is not looking? Why shouldn't I destroy that letter and say I never received it? Shall I acquire this rather good coat which nobody seems to be claiming? Or shall I set my face against all these ideas, resolutely refusing to cheat or lie or steal?

Wait a moment, it may be said. There are different sorts of wrongs. Some offences are just technical, like driving at more than thirty miles an hour in a built-up area or failing to take out a dog licence. The laws on these points are what the Government finds convenient. May that not be true of most 'wrong' actions—that they are wrong because the ruling authority which has the power to do so finds it expedient to prevent people from doing them? Now the authorities in one country may find it expedient to encourage people to do things which in another country are condemned. Officials in Nazi Germany were required to persecute certain classes of

people in ways which in most countries were considered outrageous. A Greek historian tells of an interview between a Greek and an Indian: the Indian was
as horrified to hear that the Greeks buried their fathers
as the Greek to hear that the Indians ate theirs. Does
it not look as if notions of right and wrong depend on
circumstances, as if Hamlet was right when he said,
'There's nothing good or bad but thinking makes it so'?
Perhaps moral standards are purely relative?

There is our problem. Are there fixed standards of
right and wrong?

Well, in everyday life we seem to assume that in most
things there is a right way and a wrong way. There is
a right way we reckon of playing a stroke at cricket, of
darning a sock, even of crossing the road. The right
way is the way which gives the better or more efficient
result. If you play across the ball you may well throw
your wicket away; if you just pull the hole in your sock
together anyhow you will be walking on painful lumps;
if you don't halt and look left and right you run the risk
of being run over. The proof of the right way in these
things is experience. We may do such things not in the
right way by ignorance or by wilful perversity; we find
out by experience that there is a right way and that the
wrong ways don't work. The right way takes time and
patience to learn; that may be irksome but need not
deter us. The good things in life are difficult, but once
learnt they last.

So much for dealing with things. The same applies
in the much more important matter of dealing with
people. There are certain ways of behaving towards
people which experience proves unsatisfactory, other
ways which turn out more satisfactory. I may gain an
immediate advantage over a customer by over-charging
or cheating him, but in the end I find I am the loser.
For when he finds out he will cease to trust me and to

deal with me. If I tell lies to my friend, he will give me up; if I become known for a liar, later, when I am speaking the truth, I shall not be believed. There is no security in any society whose members can't trust each other, and in the end it will break up. Society is founded on trust. I can only go on in society by assuming that I can leave things about without perpetual fear that they will be lifted, that if people promise a thing they will do it, that they mean what they say. The phrase 'honour among thieves' is an illustration of the point: a gang of thieves could not exist unless there were a mutual understanding that the members were straight with each other.

Why then should I avoid doing 'wrong'? Because it doesn't pay? That is true, and we have made a step forward when we can say that; but it is not a very satisfactory answer, because it puts right conduct on a purely mercenary basis. The implication is that, of course, if ever I find wrong *does* pay, I shall go in for it. 'Honesty is the best policy' is not a very good motto; for policy may change and then where are we?

We must therefore go deeper than that to find out why wrong is wrong. When I have seen that it is not merely a question of the consequences or of expediency, it may occur to me that wrong-doing usually comes from selfishness. If I think only of myself I may well be tempted to do what I like and to ignore the claims of others. It may occur to me that in our society I am one among many and that, if we all have equal rights and shares in our society, then I ought not as a member to do anything which I should not like all other members to do. What would be the consequences if everybody did this 'wrong'? What right have I then to do a thing which if it became universal would lead to chaos? Here again we see that wrong is anti-social, whereas right makes for harmony. Wrong then is wrong on this showing because it is contrary to man's nature as a social being. And this applies to 'technical' offences like exceeding the speed-limit in a motor-car as well as to the crimes from which we all instinctively shrink.

But this harmony extends beyond human society. The order of human society can only be reliable, a thing which you can trust, if it is thought of as harmonizing with the purpose of the universe; and, however hard it is to understand the universe, we must think of it as an ordered whole with a purpose and a plan for all its parts down to the smallest of them, if we are to think of it at all. (If there is no order in it, if it is a chaos, then it will not bear thinking about, and there is no point in asking questions about it, because there can be no answer.) Thus the Right which is necessary for society to go on is one with the Right which holds the Universe together, the sun and moon and stars and everything included. The Wrong which is the enemy of society is at variance with the true purpose of living.

Thus the ideas of right and wrong on which our laws are based are derived from standards outside the world of man. Beauty, Truth, and Goodness are not the invention of man but values revealed to him as he becomes aware of the world in which he lives. Men may see them with different eyes according to their circumstances and the environment in which they have been brought up, but substantially these values do not change. Roses die, but Beauty does not; men may act deceitfully, but the ideal of Truth remains untouched. We may be sure that it is always wrong to tell a lie or to be unkind.

Why should I hate Wrong? Because I should love Right. And why should I love Right? Because it is the Will of God who rules the universe in Right and has called me into life to share it and has revealed Himself to me in the life of Jesus Christ. To do wrong against all that—we call Sin, wrong which is an offence against God. For there are sorts of wrong which are more than mere mistakes or errors of judgement; they leave behind them a feeling of guilt; they are dirty and we have soiled ourselves in doing them and it is a sort of dirt which we cannot easily get rid of. In doing them we have not merely let down our own ideals; we have somehow let down God. I may, although I know or feel all this, still do sinful things because of my weakness, but for that I may (such is the grace of God) be forgiven. To do wrong *deliberately*, going against all that, is in the end to cut myself off from true living. Wrong hardened into chronic sin is the canker of the soul.

R. W. MOORE

What is Salvation?

I CAN, I think, best introduce this subject by telling of the conversations which I had, many years ago, with two men who had a very remarkable religious influence upon the student mind of Europe and America. One of these men secured remarkable audiences in Continental cities. A thousand men would turn out to hear him, I have been told, in Lisbon, and fifteen hundred in Vienna. He was an American and, I think, always spoke through a translator. In any case he had no natural gifts and certainly no tricks as an orator. But he spoke with obvious sincerity and in plain, lucid speech. I knew him well, and I once asked him: 'What do you say to them that makes them come to you like that?' His answer was, 'I tell them that they are enslaved, and that they know it. Then I tell them that Christ can set them free.' The other, now dead, Dr. John Kelman, had unequalled influence upon the Scottish students of his time, especially upon what is known as 'the man on the fringe', that is to say, the man who has no use for the Church, but who has his own fixed standard of fundamental decency and honour. I remember talking one night with a younger friend, a student of medicine of great distinction who had become first a Christian and then a missionary under Kelman's influence. I said to him: 'What would you say is the substance of Kelman's message?' His answer was, 'He says three things: (1) God is your Father. Live whole-heartedly in that faith. (2) There are some things that no gentleman ought to do or even think, but which it is desperately hard to avoid. (3) Only the living Christ can enable you to live daily in the Fatherhood of God, and conquer the enemy within.' Later I told this to Kelman and asked him if it was a sound statement. He was, I think, a little taken aback by the unconventional wording, but said, 'Yes, but I would put more emphasis on the third than I once did.'

Now, it is important to note that, different as was the theological outlook of my two friends, the one being a Fundamentalist and the other a Liberal, when it came to the heart of the matter they were practically at one. To both of them salvation was the attainment of filial communion with God. For both of them man as such was under an interior servitude, which prevented him from following his true destiny, and he could not alone escape from that bondage. And finally, for both alike, Jesus Christ was the one Liberator and Saviour who could deliver man from his bondage, and bring him into true communion with God, and with his fellow men. There is, of course, a great deal more in the New Testament about Salvation than that. I shall, in particular, have something to say about Salvation from Death as well as Sin. But my friends expressed the heart of the matter, and in the main I shall confine myself to their statements of the Christian message and Salvation.

The very first thing that is necessary for our true salvation is to get a true conception of God. If we have a false conception of God, then communion with Him is of no real good for man. It is quite arguable that atheism itself is better than communion with a false God. Indeed, not a little of the atheism and agnosticism in the world to-day is due to a moral revolt against false orthodoxies of traditional theologies. It is possible that these words may be read by some one who is in such temporary revolt. Agnosticism has many causes. It may have its roots in genuine perplexity as to the difficult problems set by the Universe to the thinking mind. Or it may be due to an unwillingness to surrender our lives completely to what we know to be best. In that case, owing to well-known psychological laws, the mind emits a mist which hides or discolours all the heavens and prevents us from seeing the sun in his strength. Or it may be due, as I have said, to moral revolt against a traditional theology, to which one sees no alternative except the denial that such a God exists. Or it may be all three together! In such a case what are we to do? Atheism is a pathological condition of the human spirit, and agnosticism is a confession that we are beaten! Both are profoundly unsatisfactory states of consciousness for any one who desires to keep his soul alive and to 'overcome the world'. We have in the Bible what professes to be a Revelation. That means a taking away of the 'Veil', which the Bible declares 'lies on the face of all people'. It is essential that we should at least know what the Bible contains. Let me give my results of the study of a lifetime.

It is axiomatic in the Bible that God is Sovereign over all nature and all men and women, and also that He is always morally nobler than the highest that we can even imagine. Greater than the greatest we can think, Purer and Kinder and Fairer than we can even imagine, that is the fundamental Biblical revelation of God. And in complete harmony with this revelation is its demand that therefore the sovereign duty of man is unbounded trust in God. From beginning to end the Bible calls for Faith and Obedience, and it ought so to do, if it is right in its conception of God. With this as our fundamental axiom it is our duty to sweep out of our minds all other conceptions of God as mere idols.

The whole message of the Bible is focused in Jesus of Nazareth. He and He alone gives us an adequate picture of Almighty God. Now if we would have that picture clearly before us we must go direct to the Gospels themselves. No religious books can give us the picture. We must go straight to the primitive records and let them make their own impression of the Man Himself. This takes time and labour, but is well worth while, for we are in quest of the key to the mystery of the Universe. We have to find God through finding the Man who revealed Him.

We get this best by beginning with the first three Gospels. When we have found the Man—we have to think of God in terms of the Man—God is an Almighty, All-Ruling, Eternal, Omnipresent Christ. We may put the same idea into other language. Christ reveals the Eternal Father by living the perfectly filial life, the life of full communion with God, the steady interchange of thought and affection with the Unseen Almighty Omnipresent Father, who from day to day shows Him what He wishes Him to do and meets always with an unfaltering response.

This, then, is the Father with whom we are summoned to enter into communion as the Essence of Salvation. This and nothing less than this is the Gospel, the Message and Call of God, to every human being.

Now this would be plainly impossible unless the Eternal God took and kept the initiative all the way through. This is what the Bible means by 'the Grace of God', 'the Grace of our Lord Jesus Christ'. We can, I think, from a study of the great world of Nature and from the fundamental elements in our moral and aesthetic life reach a reasoned and solid conviction as to the spiritual nature and meaning of the Universe. Personally, I think that there is a clear case for what is known as 'Natural Theology', or 'Philosophical Theism'. But what on these grounds alone we would never have reached is the assured conviction of this wonderful reality—the Grace of God. It means that, knowing every one of us through and through, the one Absolute Being has made and now makes all the advances to us, and that His great desire is to draw each of us into intimate communion of thought and heart and will with Himself, and through this union into intimate communion with all our brethren. Unless this initiative of Grace is an essential part of our thought of God we have not seen Him as Jesus Christ saw Him. Surely it has been truly said that 'he who has not seen the Grace of God as a great wonder has never seen it at all'!

This is what is involved in the faith that Jesus Christ is more than the greatest of human prophets, or interpreters of the spiritual Universe, that He is 'the Son of God', God emergent after a new fashion on the arena of time to 'seek and to *save* the lost' human race, by raising them into this trusting, loving, and obeying communion with Himself. Nor according to full Christian faith is this Supreme God confined to an Incarnation that must necessarily, as belonging to past history, become more dim and remote as the flood of Time carries us farther and farther from it. It is continued through all the ages by the coming into men's hearts of the Holy Spirit to interpret Christ, and make Him every man's living contemporary, and fill him with new moral energy and hope, and so to deliver him from the powers of that fatal inward slavery to lust and fear and care and selfishness, of which both my friends spoke; in other words, to give him full 'Salvation'. According to the New Testament we have not to make ourselves good, we have to cease from hindering God from making us good, from giving us Salvation.

I have left myself little space to write of the other great half of the good news of God in Christ, which we call the Gospel, Salvation from Death. 'Death' in the Bible is the symbol of all that tragic world of circumstance which the environment inflicts upon us, cramping and maiming the heart and mind and total life of us all, and culminating for every one of us in that death of the body which to all outward appearance extinguishes us all.

By bringing men into Communion with God through the Spirit, Christ gives them an energy of spiritual life which enables them to 'overcome the world'. This victory over the world has two stages. (1) Christians are not exempt from the shocks of fortune which are part of our human lot. But by the inward energy of life, derived from communion with God, they are enabled to surmount all these shocks of misfortune, gaining from each encounter new faith and hope and love, so that they may emerge from them richer and not poorer than before in vitality of soul, as a sea-bird rises against it by means of the very storm that would beat it down. That is the Christian ideal realized by the Master, and possible in the human degree to the disciples. The outward shocks of 'Death' drive them into the deeper impregnable fastnesses of the Love of God, to find there the energies which make them truer, kinder, humbler, wiser, and more helpful and useful men and women. 'Death' thereby becomes a means of 'Life'.

But (2) unless there is much more than this in the Gospel there is no real 'Salvation' in the full sense of the term. If literal 'Death' is what it seems to be, the complete extinction of our personalities, it is the end, also, of faith and hope and love, and Communion with God. We fight our way on through life following the Captain of our Salvation, knowing that at the end we meet with a mightier than He from whom we receive the final *coup de grâce*!

That was not the faith of the early Church. There is one saying in the New Testament of extraordinary force, which gives us some measure of the pulse of its vitality, 'Jesus Christ, who hath abolished death, and hath brought life and immortality to light through the Gospel'.[1] We have in the New Testament conception of Final Salvation, something greater than mere immor-

[1] 2 Tim. i. 10.

tality, which is a negative conception, but which includes it. Communion with God, which, as I have said, is the heart of Salvation, must necessarily have deathlessness, and the secret of endless growth in its heart. It is inconceivable that Omnipotent Love should ever let His faithful children pass out of guidance, and not rather ever desire deeper and fuller Communion with them. So, to all true Christian faith, Death itself can only be a passing incident in that Communion, the gateway to fuller life beyond, an experience which like all other experiences can be transmuted into eternal gain.

I have not touched on Social Salvation in time and in Eternity, but these are all involved in what has been already written. The conclusion of the whole matter is that Salvation according to the Bible is deliverance from the power of sin and death through Communion with the Father, as revealed by the Son through the power of the Spirit. It is begun here and it is perfected hereafter by God our Saviour.

D. S. CAIRNS

How can We be the Men God wants Us to be?

THE question assigned to me seems at first sight rather easier than some even more fundamental questions. I can, at any rate, assume that there is a God and that He cares for men. But, clearly, we must ask a preliminary question: 'What sort of people does God want us to be?' To this question the decent-living 'plain man' would probably reply: 'He wants us to be brave, unselfish, kind and ready to do our duty.' And to the next question: 'How are we to attain these qualities?' he might answer, 'Well, just by practising them, I suppose: by keeping your temper, looking for chances to help others, and so on.' That at least is the answer implied by the life he tries to live.

Now, it's true that a genuine Christian is, or should be, more brave, kind, and unselfish than one who is not a Christian. But many teachers besides Jesus—in Greece, Rome, and elsewhere—exhorted men to practise these virtues, hundreds of years before Jesus was born. Plato in Greece, for instance, and Confucius in China: and we all agree with them in our hearts. But telling a man he ought to be so and so is not the same as telling him how: and it is just at this point—the 'how'—that these great teachers seem ineffective. We may notice that their answers had little or no reference to God: the ideal they held up was man-made and man-centred. A man could make himself good, they thought, by the conscious practice of goodness. The resulting character strikes us often as what we should call a prig, full of conscious superiority and careful self-improvement. There's much that is admirable in their ideal man: but the odd thing is that the nearer the character approaches perfection, the more unattractive it is. We can see an example in the 'magnanimous man' of Aristotle, who 'confers benefits but does not receive them' because it would degrade his dignity to accept a kindness. And we can find instances nearer home. Why do we mostly feel uncomfortable on school Speech-days when we are told by eminent men that we go to school to 'strengthen and improve our characters'?

Now, of course, Christianity is profoundly concerned with our everyday behaviour and the ultimate improvement of our characters: but it does not make them ends in themselves: they are by-products. And this is right. Most of the good things in this life are by-products, and if we try to make them more than that, they wither in our grasp. Everyone knows that if you go 'all out' for popularity, you won't get it; or if you do, it won't be popularity worth having. Happiness is a deeper thing than popularity; but the child or man who says, in effect, to himself, 'I will be happy: I will be happy', won't be as happy as the one who flings himself into a job he loves, and thinks only of the job and not at all of the happiness. Our natural English suspicion of the 'prig' is a right feeling: it's a Christian feeling too. The Bible name for prig was Pharisee.

What then does Christianity put first, if it isn't the improvement of our own characters? It puts first a certain relationship to God. That will convey very little to you if you believe that the word 'God' means nothing. But the existence of the Christian's God is not what I am asked to discuss: I take it for granted. How then are we to picture this relationship? If there be a God, he is a unique being. We can't properly compare our attitude to Him with anything else. We can only make pictures of it, more or less inadequate. What then is the picture by which we can best make real to our minds the relation of a man to God, when the man wants to become what God intended him to be? It's not the picture of a man training himself by ceaseless effort to get a little nearer his own ideal standard; nor is it the picture—favoured by the Stoics—of a brave man standing defiant and alone, though the world is crashing in ruins around him.

The picture will be more that of a well waiting to be filled by the rain: a wire connected up with some inexhaustible supply of current: a statue waiting to come alive. Such a picture may strike you as less 'natural' than the others (indeed it's not natural; it's supernatural). But it's nearer the truth of Christianity.

So far we have only answered the question in the roughest, most general way, by saying that the Christian's first duty is to stand in right relationship with God, and that the attitude should be more that of receiving than of initiating. Study of the Bible and the experience of Christians through the centuries may help us to fill in the background.

There are certain keywords in the understanding of Christianity: and to trace their use through the Bible is a good foundation for Christian conviction: words like Truth, Light, Mercy. I think the keyword for our present purpose is 'Father'. The most adequate picture we can get to illustrate the relation between Man and God is the picture of children and a father. That means, of course, in the first place that our attitude should be one of trustfulness, intimacy, and respect. That has been the subject of many sermons. But Christianity goes farther. It does not only tell us to regard God as a fatherly sort of person, who will be just and patient and loving. It tells us something much more mysterious. It says that just as we are physically the sons of our human fathers, so we are spiritually sons of God. However we behave, however much we ignore our inheritance, we are God's children. The New Testament does not hesitate to use the word 'begotten', which is a different word from 'created'. Any man can create something, in the sense of 'making' it: only a father can beget, and what he begets is potentially something like himself. What we inherit from our parents forms the groundwork of our characters: we may, of course, ignore it, deface it, or—our human parents being imperfect creatures—improve on it. But it remains the source and basis of our natural life. And, the nearer we keep to our parents as we grow up, the more we shall be influenced by them. The spiritual life, for Christians, runs parallel to the natural human life. It is in us potentially from the first: we can forget it, or spoil it: most of us do. But it is there; and by recognizing it and fostering it by all the means we can, we shall have, as St. John says, the power, the right, the privilege to be fully sons of God. That, and nothing less than that, is the sort of people God wants us to be.

There are some splendid promises in the Bible about the happiness of this condition once we begin to achieve it: the sense of power, the feeling of trust, the unself-conscious ease of being 'at home' which only member-ship of a family can give us.

Of course it isn't all plain sailing: we must be educated in sonship. We shall often fail to live up to our in-heritance: the obstacles will be many and painful, most often the obstacles of our own failings; and no education is wholly painless. But the nearer we get to the true sense of being children in the home, the less will the pains of the outside world be able to keep us back. We know that God has appointed ways in which we can keep alive in us the memory of our sonship and by which we can become more nearly what we were intended to be: Study of His Word, Prayer, and Sacra-ment. Most people in Britain to-day make no use at all of these means of approach, and would tell you they

mean nothing whatever to them. They are entitled to
their opinion: but they are not entitled to criticize the
Christian way of life, as they do, without even having
tried the appointed paths that lead us on to it.

Are there then no conditions which we must accept
if we are to enjoy this consciousness of being the children
of God? There is certainly one, and it is fundamentally
important. We are not in the position of 'only children';
we are members of a family. And the one condition
which the Father of the family makes about his love and
our right of sharing it is that we shall, to the best of
our power, love the other members of the family, as He
does. This after all is the condition of any successful
family-life. But it's not a thing that comes naturally
to most children. It has to be trained. Many sons
begin by wanting to make a 'corner' in their parents'
affection, and are even ready to keep the others out by
criticizing them and thinking ill of them.

This, I take it, is the real point of the parable of the
Prodigal Son, perhaps the most penetrating parable that
Jesus ever spoke. The point for us is quite as much the
sulkiness of the elder brother as the repentance of the
prodigal. The elder brother has been the 'good boy':
he thinks that this gives him a special claim to his
father's affection. The father's answer is that this
attitude is just the one thing which is bound to frustrate
the love which the father is eager to show to the whole
family. The parable is a perfect picture of what
Christians say to God every day in the Lord's Prayer:
'forgive our sins against you as we forgive the sins of
others against us.'

It is along these lines that I should answer the
question: 'How can we be the men God wants us to
be?'—not by making efforts which begin and end in
ourselves, but by remembering what we have it in us
to become, through our inheritance. I can imagine

some readers not thinking this 'practical' enough and altogether too religious and mysterious. But I believe it is the weakness of the British in their religion to make too much of their own conduct and not enough of God's grace; and when they find, quite rightly, that pre-occupation with their own conduct makes them self-centred, they put it down to 'religion' and go no farther with it.

The beginning of Religion is not with ourselves but with God. There are appointed and accepted ways of approaching God: Prayer, Sacrament, and study of the Bible; and they are all most unfashionable to-day. But no one said that Christianity was fashionable or ever professed to be. It is much more fashionable to say, 'I've no use for Religion.' If we do say that, it is we that are being judged, not Religion. Only a small minority of the world even tries 'to be the men God wants them to be': but it's a minority numbering many thousands of people among whom are some of the most effective and heroic characters of whom we have any record. None of them found the Christian way to fail them, once they had honestly tried it. Most of the critics have not even tried it. How many of us have?

J. T. CHRISTIE

How is it Possible for us to be like Our Lord Jesus Christ?

I

I HAVE been asked to write something about certain questions which, I am told, a good many of the members of your club have been asking. What is the meaning of those words of Jesus in Matthew v. 48: 'Be ye therefore perfect, as your Father which is in heaven is perfect'? What is the good of telling a man to be perfect when he knows well enough that it is impossible? Again: Of what use is it to aim at likeness to Christ, who was sinless, when one is fully aware that one is sinful oneself, and so does not, so to say, start fair? Lastly: Even if one does aim at being as like Christ as one can, with however little hope of more than a very slight degree of success in the attempt, will not one become an unmanly, priggish sort of fellow, who will only be despised by his companions who are ready to enjoy life and get the best out of it that they can, in the way of pleasure and adventure?

II

Now, first about the words of Jesus in Matthew v. 48: 'Be ye therefore perfect, as your Father which is in heaven is perfect.' We are often far too much inclined to take texts in the Bible all by themselves, out of their context and apart from the occasion on which they were spoken or written. But this is not the way to understand any book. If, in this case, we look at the rest of the passage in which these words occur we shall find that they are not really so unpractical as to require of you and me that we should try to be as 'perfect', in the sense of being as completely and faultlessly good, as God our heavenly Father. Jesus has just been speaking of people who said that it was right to love one's friends, but that one need not love one's enemies; and he says, on the other hand, that this is a very poor, improper sort of love; not like God's love, who sends sunshine and rain on good and evil alike. Any one, he reminds us, can love their friends and do good to them; but we ought to imitate the love of God, which is a perfect or complete love, an 'all-round' love, as we might say, because it does not limit itself to the good people who love him, but extends to the bad people who do not love him. It is of this 'perfect' or all-round love which is not only for those who return it, as compared with the 'imperfect', one-sided love which insists on gratitude and what we call a *quid pro quo*, that Jesus is here speaking; it is not about being 'perfect' in the sense of particularly good. And even about this command to love bad men and enemies as well as good men and friends, a word of explanation is needed. For a man may reasonably ask whether he can possibly love his enemies as well as he loves his friends. He must then bear in mind that the word which is here translated 'love' does not mean feeling affection such as one may have for one's mother, or for one's intimate friend, or for the girl one is, as we say, 'in love with'. One cannot command people to feel affection, because they cannot feel affection to order. Nor can any one be expected to have a feeling of affection for every one he knows, still less for people whom he does not know. But the word translated 'love' here means a will to do to others as we would wish them to do to us—to treat them as well as if we loved them in the other sense. We find, indeed, by experience, that if we behave to people as if we liked them we generally come to like them—certainly to like them more than we should have done if we had indulged our feelings of dislike toward them and treated them accordingly. The enemies whom we treat as fairly and kindly as we should treat our friends will often end in becoming our friends. In any

case it is this goodwill towards our enemies, this fair and
kind treatment of them, that is meant when Jesus tells us
to love our enemies; the word which is used in the
original Greek is a different word from that which would
be used to mean personal affection. This is not whittling
down the difficulty of being a good Christian. It is really
very hard to treat all men as you would wish them to
treat you without unfairly favouring those whom you
like and taking it out of those whom you do not like. It
is very hard, and it is well worth doing; but it is not impossible, as it would be to *feel* to those who treat you
badly as you do to those who are near and dear to you.
In bidding us love our enemies our Lord Jesus Christ
sets us a difficult task, but not an impossible one. And we
must remember that He Himself showed us the way. We
are told that when He hung on the cross He prayed for
His murderers; and the Apostle Paul says that it was while
we were still sinners that He gave us the supreme proof of
love in dying for us.

III

Now I will say something about the imitation of Christ
which is recommended to us. Christians have always
believed their Master to have been without sin, but they
have never supposed that they could imitate Him in this.
On the contrary, they have for the most part thought
that we begin our lives, so to speak, under a handicap
which He was without, an inherited tendency to go
wrong which they called 'original sin'. Nor, of course,
have they supposed that we are bound to imitate Him in
the circumstances of His earthly life; to be all of us
carpenters by trade, as He was, for example, or to give
up our trade, as He did, in order to preach the Gospel, or
to remain like Him unmarried and without a fixed home.
The imitation of Christ which is recommended to us is
an imitation of that whole-hearted obedience to our

heavenly Father and of that self-sacrificing service of our fellow men of which His earthly life was so splendid a pattern. Yet on that account to despair of following Him at all would be as foolish as to give up trying to be as good as we can at a game, or at playing a musical instrument, or at any other pursuit, because we do not expect ever to be equal to the most famous performers. We shall do all the better for pitching our standard as high as possible, and not being content till we have come as near it as we can; but nearer than that we cannot come, and no one can blame us if we have done our best. There is, however, one thing to be said about taking Christ as our standard and pattern of living which cannot be said in the same way as taking the great football-players or musicians or political leaders whom we should like to resemble as nearly as we can for our standard and pattern in those particular ways of living, football-playing, music, or politics. For we have the word of millions of men and women that in our efforts to follow Christ we can find help to do so if only we seek it regularly and faithfully in prayer and communion, not giving up the search because it does not at once succeed, but going on and on, like the widow of the parable, who got what she wanted out of the unjust judge by sheer persistence in asking. God, however, is not like the unjust judge who cared nothing about those who came to him for protection till they had worried him into doing something for the sake of a quiet life. He *does* care about us, and just for that reason He often puts our love and faith to the test. But we must remember that, however hard our trial, it will never be harder than that which Jesus Himself underwent when, while dying on the cross, He felt Himself deserted by His heavenly Father and cried out: 'My God, my God, why hast thou forsaken me?'

Thus this imitation or following of Christ which is recommended to us is to be understood neither as a vain pursuit of an unattainable perfection, nor even as an attempt to come as near as we can by our own unaided efforts to the high standard which our Lord has set us; but as an endeavour to come as near as we can to that standard which has been put into our minds by God and carried through from beginning to end by the power of what we call the 'grace of God'—a spiritual force which comes to us through Christ Himself and which, if we let it work in us, will make us over again, as it were, in His likeness.

IV

But, supposing all this to be true, some of you may after all not be too sure that you want to be made over again in the likeness of Christ. You may be inclined to fancy that this would mean being made into something priggish and unmanly and being cut off from the enjoyments and adventures of life. I will end by trying to show that it is a great mistake to fancy anything of the sort.

No one was ever less what is called a 'prig' than was Jesus our Master during His life on earth. He was called 'a glutton and a winebibber' because He was so ready to go into cheerful company, and there were pious people who thought that He was none too careful about the character of those with whom He associated. The idea which some have that a Christian life consists in *not* doing certain things—drinking and smoking, for example— and looking down on those who do them—does not come from the Gospels. Jesus, as I have just reminded you, was not afraid of drinking wine—smoking was not invented in those days, but there is no reason to suppose that, if it had been, He would have disapproved of it. He was not married, indeed, and He blessed those who gave up the hope of marrying that they might have more leisure to preach the good news of the kingdom of God; but He blessed marriage too, and spoke of it as instituted

N

by God. So it may be right for a man to give up drinking
drinks which, if we take too much of them, may make us
lose control of ourselves and neglect those who depend
upon us. We may find it hard to stop ourselves from
taking too much, if we once begin; and it is often easier to
have a rule of taking none than to keep ourselves within
bounds when we have taken some. Or, again, it may be
that our giving up such drinks may help others to keep
straight; and it is certainly acting more like Christ to give
up a pleasure for the sake of helping others than to stick
to what one enjoys oneself at the risk of doing others
harm. Moreover, such pleasures as eating and drinking
are always best enjoyed not for their own sake and alone
but as part of cheerful social intercourse with our friends.
But they are good in their place; and, even if we give
them up for good reasons, we shall be giving up what is
good for the sake of what is better; and to call them bad
pleasures because they may be bad for us, so that we do
right in giving them up, is to behave like the fox in the
fable, who called the grapes sour because he could not
get at them. And, to say one word about those other
pleasures which go with marriage, we are to keep ourselves pure and refuse to indulge in those pleasures until
we are married, not because they are bad in themselves,
but because to indulge in them for our selfish pleasure
cheapens them and cannot be done without treating ourselves and others as if we were mere animals, and not as if
we were human beings who are able to use our bodily
appetites, as the animals cannot, as instruments in living
a higher kind of life, which we call a spiritual life; a life
of love to God and to our fellow men, in which there is
nothing to be ashamed of, nothing which we are not glad
should come to the light and into the presence of God, of
whom we are told that He is light and in Him is no darkness at all.

The man who always keeps himself in touch with

Christ will not live a duller or emptier life than the man who lets his religion go. He will use his mind, for he will always be distinguishing between what is right and what is wrong to do. He will be master of himself, not carried away by the desire of the moment, and will have a fuller and more adventurous life than those who let themselves be so carried away, because his eyes will always be fixed on something better than the present, and he will never be content with himself as he is, but will ever be looking for new opportunities of serving and doing good to others and of making his own life and, if possible, that of his town and his country and the whole world better than he found it and more fit to be part of that kingdom of God which Christ came to set up among men.

CLEMENT C. J. WEBB

Why do You believe in the Church and how can It help You?

WHY do I believe in the Church? First, let me make it as plain as I can what the Church is—which may be something quite different from what you think it is, especially if you are one of those who say they have no use for the Church. What, then, is it? I believe that Jesus Christ came to us to start something—to bring God to us and us to God in a new and deeper way. He did all that God could do in a human life to show God's true character and to bring us to Him: and He handed on His work to those who believe in Him. That's the Church—Jesus Christ and those who believe in Him. As any earthly society must, it has an organization— He built it round His Apostles: He gave it officers, basic facts, and principles (what we now call the Creed), symbolic acts like the Holy Communion (the point of which is that they are His actions as well as ours, we meet Him in them), and He gave it a job to do. Now, however much of a mess we Christians make of it, the Church is Christ's: it's His show: I believe in it, because I believe in Him. There's a whole section of it, the biggest part, I can't see at all—the Church beyond; it has not got our earthly organization any longer: it has its own job to do in heaven. But we belong to-gether, we are part of it—because Christ is the Lord of all life in God here and hereafter. And let me say frankly, there are, no doubt, many in the Church above who missed their way into the Church on earth, and members of the Church here who have missed the way into the Church above. The final test, as our Lord said, is what you are and what you have done as you stand before God's judgement seat.

Well, there is the Church—as Christ made it. Of course I believe in it. It is just the operative Body of Christ Himself.

Now let's come to the Church as you and I see it organized here on earth, with its many divisions and differences. It's nowhere near up to Christ's idea of the Church or up to the work He gave it to do. That's obvious. But still I believe in it: it is a necessity of Christian life. It's got the things Christ entrusted to it: it's got the same structure of continuous life, the same basic faith and principles enshrined in the creeds, the same sacred actions or sacraments, the same job. If I believe in Christ and want to do a job for Him and let Him do a job for me, of course I must be inside, not outside, the Church. And by the Church here I mean all the different Christian Churches: we differ on some things; but we agree on far more things, and we are beginning to work together. The Church is sometimes better and sometimes worse at its job. But, there's no one else to do the job: for only the Church has the tradition, the faith, the tools, which Christ gave it. And it is not doing its job so badly either: in every country of the world it is bringing men to God and is the hard core of resistance to the degrading forces of the world, the flesh, and the devil. O yes, I believe in it and if you want to serve Christ your place is inside it too.

How can it help you to believe in the Church? If what I said above is true, the Church is there to do a job and Christ put it there and you won't be putting your back into Christian life and work unless you are a joined member of it. How will the Church help you? Well, first it will train you to know what Christ has told us about God and Himself, about yourself and all men, about this world and the next. That is Christian doctrine or teaching. The Church is built not on what

we feel or suppose, but on what by God's grace we
know—there are, of course, things we don't understand, but we know enough to walk by. Secondly, the
Church helps you to act accordingly, after Christ's
example. That's discipline. There are things a
Christian must not do and he knows it: there are things
he ought to do and he knows it. To fail is to let Christ
down and the Church. And the Church helps you not
merely to know God or to try to obey Him—but in a
real way to see Him, to love Him, to trust Him, and to
receive from Him strength of spirit, beyond any
strength of ours, to be in heart and life a Christian.
It's that kind of thing in another way that the Army
does for a recruit—it trains him to think and act as a
soldier—but all the time to *be* a soldier. Well, the
Church trains you to think and act as a disciple of
Christ, but all the time to *be* at heart true to Him. In
doing that the Church brings into use spiritual muscles
which otherwise you would never use at all: when the
Church comes together to worship God, we use a
common drill—confession of our sins and of all the
evil done under the sun, thanksgiving for God's goodness, prayer for ourselves and all sorts and conditions
of men, and that humble reverence before the mystery
and wonder of God's love and holiness which we call
worship. We've all got those spiritual muscles: the
Church trains us to use them. If we don't belong to
a Church or the Church, we miss the doctrine, the
discipline, the drill, all the encouragement of companionship with others in the service of Christ, and so
we miss Christ perhaps altogether: for remember the
Church is Christ among His disciples.

If you say, 'Well, the church I know isn't like that,
it's dead-alive and has got no kick in it and no use for
me, nor me for it'—I'm sorry. It is like that sometimes.
But more often than you think, if you're looking for the

right thing, you'll find it there. How does the Church help me? It helps me to follow Christ. Outside the Church I'm a straggler, half-hearted, perhaps a traitor. Inside I'm one of His Company, and I learn from Him and from it more than I can ever give.

GEOFFREY CANTUAR:

Does a Christian need to go to Church?

A CHRISTIAN does need to go to church, for many reasons. One of the principal reasons for going is to say his prayers. For a church is above all a house of prayer, and how charmingly Coleridge has pictured it to us:

> To walk together to the kirk,
> And all together pray,
> While each to his great Father bends,
> Old men, and babes, and loving friends,
> And youths and maidens gay.

You can, of course, say your prayers in other places, and I hope you do. A Christian, surely, is the first to realize that the whole of life belongs to God, and that prayers in church can never be a substitute for prayers in private, any more than your piety on Sunday can give you leave to do as you like during the rest of the week.

It is true that there are people who sometimes make an unreal separation between prayer and life, between Sunday and Monday. For example, there is Mr. Pump, delightfully sketched for us by Mr. A. A. Milne in his novel, *Two People*:

'Mr. Pump', writes Mr. Milne, 'was not a hypocrite. He was a religious man, whose religion was too sacred a thing to be carried into his business. The top-hat that he hung up in his office was not the top-hat that he prayed into before placing it, thus hallowed, between his feet, even if the frock-coat and the aspect of benevolence were the same. He had two top-hats, and one hat-box for them. On the Monday morning he put God reverently away for the week and took out Mammon. On the Sunday morning he came back—gratefully or hopefully, according to business done—to God. No man can serve two masters simultaneously.'

It is not hard to find Mr. Pumps in the world, with their

prayers and piety one day a week. There have always been, and perhaps always will be, plenty of them. There is a saying so old that its spelling is in Middle English, and Spenser, who records it, says it was an old saying even in his day: 'To kerke the narre, from God more farre'; or, as we should put it to-day, 'The nearer the church, the farther from God.' But that is not really true, so wise old Matthew Henry put the proverb in another form: 'It is common for those that are farthest from God to boast themselves most of their being near to the Church.'

It is not good for a Christian to boast about anything: 'By their works shall ye know them', said Jesus, and we may venture to hope that our lives will be so sincere and true that men may know that we have been with Jesus. But we shall not come nearer to Him by leaving the Church. What we should aim at, for the Church is the Body of Christ, is to be near the Church and also near to God; and if we are really near the Church we shall be near to God. Jesus once said, 'I will build my Church'. We may be sure He did not propose to build it for no reason. He built the Church that through it He might be with His people always. So it is good for us to remember, as George Herbert reminds us, that 'Once thy foot enters the church . . . God is more there than thou'. In other words, if we go there to find God we shall not be disappointed; He is more really present than we ourselves.

You have heard it said, no doubt, that you can worship God in the open air; some go so far as to say that you can worship Him better there. As Browning once asked,

> Why, where's the need of Temple, when the walls
> O' the world are that?

Well, there is just this need of a temple, that while you can say your prayers in the open air, you do not often do it. We are creatures of habit, and habits are very useful,

provided that they are the right kind. And if we make it
a habit to meet God where men have long been accustomed to meet Him, it helps us; and that is one reason
why going to church helps us. For what makes a church
a holy place? Is it the moderator's or bishop's consecration? No, that is only a symbolical and representative
act. What really makes a church a holy place is that week
by week and day by day men have met God there, offered
their prayers and adoration, and have heard Him speak
authentic truth to their hearts and wills.

But I am not at all sure that when we go hiking into the
country, or cycling, or by a bus or train, that we often
meet God. It is not that we cannot, but rather that we
do not. We do enjoy His sunshine and His hills, the song
of the birds, and the flowers in the meadows, the splash
and fall of the burn in the glen. And sometimes, when we
are in a poetic mood, they do draw us close to God. Nature has that power, and we should school ourselves to be
open to its influence, as Jesus always was. Yet that does
not detract from the truth that, speaking generally, when
we go to the country we do not go to say our prayers but
to have a jolly time.

Actually, however, there is no reason why these two
things, going to the country and going to church, should
ever be set over against each other. Why not do both?
Once again our Lord is our pattern and example here.
'As his custom was,' we read, 'he went into the synagogue
on the sabbath day.' Our Lord knew the value of common prayer and of the communal hearing of God's
Word; these together built up a life until it was hid in
God. So our Lord made a habit on the sabbath day of
going to the house of prayer and fellowship.

But that was not all; for what do we read in another
place? There is this record: 'And it came to pass that
he went through the corn fields on the sabbath day.' It
upset the strict Pharisees when they saw Him doing this,

especially when His disciples began to pluck the ears of corn and grind them between their hands, blowing away the chaff and eating the corn. So the Pharisees took Jesus to task on that point. And He replied, 'The sabbath was made for man, and not man for the sabbath.' But Jesus didn't say, The sabbath was made for fun; enjoy yourself to the limit. Nor did He mean that. He meant something that goes much deeper: that the sabbath was a day not so much of recreation as of re-creation. And, as His own example showed, part of the re-creation might well consist in out-door exercise, a walk in the country; but another part lay in going, 'as his custom was', to the worship of Almighty God. The sabbath was a day not merely for the refreshment of the body and mind; it was a day also for the refreshment of the spirit, a refreshment that can come only out of communion with the living God. Our Lord's own practice is the best commentary to His words.

On the other hand, I must readily, if unhappily, grant you that many, too many, of our churches to-day are pretty gloomy and forbidding, places 'where everything combines to make one dismal', as a popular novelist has recently said. But that is not what a church should be like; it should be a place where everything combines to make one joyous, for what can be a more joyous experience than the worship of God. If a church is a dismal place it is because of the neglect of its people. Often it is a sincere neglect, born of misunderstanding, of the queer idea that beauty and light disturb and distract, while ugliness and gloom minister to reverence. This lugubrious muddle-headedness is perhaps enough to drive youth from our churches, but we may hope that the reaction will be of another kind. That youth, with its splendid power of harnessing action to vision, will not forsake the churches, but on the contrary will insist upon them being made finer and more beautiful, fitting houses for the worship of God. Let the vigour and enthusiasm of our youth, seeing visions of what our churches might be, shape a nobler tradition in our day for the generations yet to come. A shirker or a coward might turn aside and say the task is too heavy, but the man with courage in his heart inspired by love of the Master will gladly hazard his life upon the venture.

There is yet another reason why a Christian needs to go to church, and that is to hear God's Word. Not only do we speak with God; He speaks with us. We hear His voice in Scripture and in sermon, our wills are moved, and our hearts are strengthened. Again and again we need to hear the old, old story, that we may take it in. In private we must read and study too, but the public hearing of God's Word is a unique experience, strangely persuasive and enheartening. No substitute can quite take its place.

But, most of all, a Christian needs to go to church because it is there he meets the risen living Lord. There is a promise never broken: 'Where two or three are gathered together in my name, there am I in the midst of them.' So conscious and so certain were Christians of this that they abandoned the sabbath, the seventh day of the week, and worshipped on the first day of the week, calling it the Lord's day because it was the day on which He rose triumphant and ever-living from the dead. And so eager were they to meet Him that they began their worship before daybreak, in order to be ready to receive Him at the hour of His resurrection when He first appeared to Mary. How beautiful it all was; how beautiful we could keep it still. No wonder Christians stood when the Gospel was read: their King was speaking to them, and their King was there. The Lord's day, not the sabbath day, became their day of worship; and it was a day of worship above all else. They might have their ordinary work to do, but first they would worship God in Christ, their living and triumphant Lord.

And all this is most abundantly and surely true when we meet on the first day of the week, as the early Christians always did, for the celebration of Holy Communion, that feast of life and gladness, when we show forth the death of a risen Lord. As our Westminster Directory declares, it 'is frequently to be celebrated'. John Calvin, our greatest Reformer, was even more explicit: 'At the very least', he wrote, 'once a week Holy Communion should be celebrated in the Christian congregation.'

WILLIAM D. MAXWELL

Isn't Christianity 'played out'?

LET's look at it this way: 'From that time many of his disciples went back and walked no more with him. Then said Jesus unto the Twelve, "Will ye also go away?" Then Simon Peter answered him, "Lord, to whom shall we go? Thou hast the words of eternal life " '[1] You see, the occasion was a critical one. Jesus had gathered round him a popular following. But he was well aware that the motives that inclined many to accept his leadership were the wrong ones; that few of his disciples understood his purpose and none its implications. So he challenged his followers; and many decided that he was not their man. They left him; and the inner circle of his chosen disciples watched their support dwindle away. No doubt they were uneasy and alarmed; for not only was the tide turning against them; they had heard their leader deliberately courting the disaster. The shadow of defeat fell upon them and chilled their spirits. Jesus felt it, too; he turned to them and asked, 'Well! Are you going, too?' It was, we may say, the first crisis in the history of Christianity, on which the future depended. Simon Peter, the fisherman, decided it; and their hesitation and disappointment can be felt in his answer, 'Lord! to whom shall we go? Thou hast the words of eternal life.'

That was a long time ago—nearly two thousand years. A few months later the defeat had reached its climax. The religious and secular authorities put an end to his preaching: the people he had disappointed hounded him to his death: the inner circle of his disciples forsook him and fled, and Simon Peter, for all his impulsive loyalty, denied with oaths and curses that he had ever known the man. Another rebel against the

[1] John vi. 66–8.

sacred tradition had been silenced: another disturber of the Roman peace had been finally eliminated. Even to the few who had clung to him in desperation it was the end.

Yet in truth it was only the beginning. It was not the final defeat of a local revolt against authority: it was the most spectacular and significant victory in the annals of human history. This is the plain verdict of the facts. For two years or three, Jesus went about the villages of Palestine speaking to obscure people: then, because what he said seemed dangerous to the authorities, he was put to death. To-day, we count history backwards and forwards from him: rightly—for whatever else may be doubtful, and however we may seek to explain it, he had changed the course of history. In a real sense history began with Jesus: not, indeed, the story of the vicissitudes of human experience, the record of the rise and fall of cultures and nations; but history as a continuity of action and purpose, which moves now before our eyes towards the unification of mankind. The living forces which are shaping the destiny of the world have their roots in Christendom; and Christendom, both Eastern and Western, is the creation of the Christian churches. Behind it all, as the seed from which it has grown, is the life and teaching of Jesus.

It may be said that this is to claim too much. Is there any significant sense in which one man can be singled out as pre-eminently the artificer of the destiny of mankind? The very idea is preposterous. At the most we can allow that in course of time Jesus became the central figure in the religion of Europe; and elaborate ritual and a vast body of mystical doctrine was built round his memory. The fragments of it still linger on among us, but the march of history is flowing beyond them and leaving them behind—the wrecks and relics of an ancient priestcraft. Surely that is all there is to it, if we appeal to history?

I think not; I believe that such an account misses the whole point. Even in the life of individuals, what unity and continuity are achieved depend upon an aim clearly perceived and constantly pursued. The continuity of history since Jesus is of this kind. It moves to a goal, more and more clearly envisaged; sustained by transcending motives constantly renewed. The progress which marks the history of Christendom is no process of natural evolution. It is not characteristic of human society as a whole. It depends now, and has always depended, in the last resort, upon men for whom the meaning of their own lives has become the realization of the human brotherhood, in whom the natural motives have been transformed by the vision of a world to be saved by their own sacrifice. It was this vision and this transformation that came into the world with Jesus.

It was no accidental result of his moral teaching. Indeed, Jesus was no moralist—neither Eastern sage nor Greek philosopher. He was a man sent on a mission with a work to do, a task to accomplish. There is nothing of the mystic visionary or the inspired dreamer about him. On the contrary, he is intensely practical and overwhelmingly deliberate. He is sent to proclaim the good news of the coming of the Kingdom of Heaven. That is the purpose of God and therefore the objective for Man—the meaning of human life. Since it is the purpose of God it will be achieved. Since it is the purpose of God, it is in some sense the natural objective of all men. But it is not the actual objective of ordinary living. How then is the real issue to be faced? How can the springs of action in men and women be transformed? The radical transformation of the motives that determine the relationships of men in society to one another—that is the problem as Jesus saw it; and to this his life was devoted. How can man be born again; redeemed from sin; re-made into a new creation?

That was the question Jesus set for himself and for mankind. He thought of himself as the Sower, sowing the tiny seed that would grow into a great tree and fill the whole earth. The ground had been prepared—so he saw the history that lay behind him. Now he had been sent to sow the seed broadcast that would spring up and grow where it found good soil. He undertook the task; pondered the conditions of accomplishing it; rejected with complete realism all the seductive short-cuts that would prove blind alleys, and fulfilled the conditions with unflinching determination. 'The seed', he said, 'is the Word.' Not the idea in the mind, which has neither hands nor feet, but the living word which is the self-expression of an inner integrity. He realized also the condition of its creativeness. 'Except a corn of wheat fall into the ground and die, it abideth alone.'

This was the task which Jesus took upon himself and to which with full consciousness he limited himself—to sow the seed of the transformation of human motives. If you would ask whether his mission was a success or a failure, you must ask only this question, 'Are there signs, in the centuries that have passed since his mission was complete, that the seed is growing, that it is bearing fruit in the creation of a new spirit in the relations of men, in a transformation of human motives?' No other question is to the point; and to this question the answer is undoubtedly 'Yes'. You can read the answer in the bitterness of his enemies and in the growing fury of their oppositions; in Frederick Nietzsche, for instance. You can hear it in the testimony of a great multitude throughout the ages—and to-day they are to be found in every nation under the sky—who bear witness to a transformation of the springs of life in themselves. From Paul of Tarsus to the last convert in modern China or Nigeria—men and women of all races and classes and cultures, they talk of him not as a great thinker or sage or moralist—but in strange, intimate terms—as their saviour or their redeemer, as a master who is a friend—as someone who has done for them something so miraculous that they can only express it by worshipping him as the incarnation of the Creator of Heaven and Earth. Of that great cloud of witnesses few have not faced the evidence of defeat and echoed the words of Simon Peter: 'Lord! to whom shall we go? Thou hast the words of eternal life.'

A great company—Yes. But what have they done and what are they doing to save the world? Even if we grant that many have in the past found Christianity a refuge and a consolation for their individual frustrations, what does it all amount to? We are living in a world which walks in the shadow of death. Two world wars have come near to ending the civilization that the Church built up. We look forward with anxiety to an even greater cataclysm; hoping to be saved from it, but without a solid ground for the hope. If ever the world needed salvation it is now. We all know it; though we try not to think about it. Does anyone really think that Christianity can save the world now? We must listen to the growing multitude of honourable, earnest, and thoughtful voices which answer, 'No.' Especially we must attend to the verdict of those—and they are not few—who work and sacrifice to achieve the very brotherhood of man that Jesus proclaimed, and for whom Christianity is at best a blunted instrument and at the worst the centre and symbol of all they fight against.

What do these men say?

They say: Christianity is dope. Behind its fine phrases and high sentiments about human brotherhood there is an ugly reality. When has the Church been the leader of the oppressed against their oppressors? Has she not always supported worldly authority, however unjust and extortionate, against those who strove for freedom and justice? She has preached the virtues of poverty while she amassed wealth; inculcated humility while her prelates became a byword for pride. She has fought in the van of the struggle against the freedom of the human spirit, against enlightenment, against science. She has talked peace, and blessed war. When her own power or prestige has been threatened no policy has been too machiavellian, no weapon too inhuman for use in its defence. When she had the power, she tortured and slew all those who dared, for conscience' sake, to oppose her claims. Now that her power is gone, she must use other methods; but at heart she remains the same—the last refuge of superstition, bigotry, obscurantism, and reaction. That is your Church!—a façade of fair words that cover an inward rottenness.

That is what they say. What is the answer? There is no honest answer except that it is true: that it is not the whole truth does not make it false. Yet it is not surprising: for such has been the predominant character of established religions everywhere and at all times. Neither is it new: the whole diatribe is an echo from the past. You will find it in the twenty-third chapter of St. Matthew's gospel, the verdict of Jesus upon the established religion of his time. The accusations are the same—only the language is different; more passionate, more bitterly contemptuous. To this day the words sting and burn; and the bitterest enemies of religion in our day have never approached the lyrical fury of his denunciation. ('Ye compass sea and land to make one convert; and when he is made ye make him twofold more the child of hell than yourselves. . . . Blind guides! which strain at a gnat and swallow a camel! . . . Whited sepulchres, . . . outwardly beautiful, . . . full of dead men's bones.')

It is a mistake to imagine that the battle for Christianity is a fight between the Church and the world. It goes on both in the Church and in the world. It is no struggle of creeds or of institutions: its battle-ground is in the minds and hearts of men and women. Christianity, in truth, is the impact of Jesus—of his life and teaching—upon the world, and the slow transformation of human motives that is the continuing result of that impact. The Christian Church, even at its worst, has been, and will long remain, the medium through which the story of Jesus and the record of his teaching are kept operative in the world. However she may wrap them up in mysterious philosophy; or render them almost indecipherable with glosses and interpretations; however her acts and policies, her ignorance or her cowardice, may belie her profession; she must perform this service to mankind, or collapse in mockery and derision. No greater service has ever been done by any human organization than this; and upon the fulfilment of this task the salvation of the world depends. If to-day there are men who labour to realize the human brotherhood, turning their backs on Christianity and building on other foundations—that in itself is evidence of the transformation of human motives and human objectives that has already been made effective: and the standards by which they judge and condemn Christianity are themselves the measure of the Christian influence.

In our time multitudes have turned from Christianity to find other leaders who would offer short cuts to the promised land. They have looked to science and to the techniques that science has made possible. They have turned to political programmes for the reorganization of society. They have put their trust in power. Their power has turned the world into a bedlam; science has given them the atomic bomb; the statesmen move from deadlock to deadlock. One thing at last is so clear that it has become a commonplace. Unless the fear and suspicion that frustrate all efforts to reconcile the nations can be dissipated, the outcome must be a convulsion of the world before which the imagination quails. This is the issue on which everything hangs— the transformation of human motives. This was the issue that Jesus faced, and to which he offered a solution. He began a process which has slowly but surely worked to transform the motives of men in their relations with one another. I know of no other force that operates in the world in this way and to this end. And so—as I see many going away to other leaders or to none, and the shadow of defeat falling upon the Christian cause, I am dismayed and filled with doubt. Yet in spite of everything, I can only stand with Simon Peter. When I hear in my heart the question, 'Will you also go away?', I can only answer as he did: 'Lord, to whom shall we go? Thou hast the words of eternal life.'

JOHN MACMURRAY

What are We to make of the Old Testament?

HOW is the Old Testament relevant to us, and what help can we find in it? Certainly there are very many to-day who do not know what to make of the Old Testament. But is it certain that this is anything to be proud of? Great-grandfather had a deep reverence for it, loved its wonderful stories, used it to stir up in him thoughts of God's Righteousness, and praised God in the words of its psalms. If we, when we think of the Old Testament, think first of the blood-thirstiness of Jael in killing Sisera and of Saul in exterminating the Amalek-ites, or reflect that there never was a Garden of Eden, and that the story of Adam and Eve is not literally true, it is possible that the comparison between us and great-grandfather does not do us credit.

I am, of course, being unfair. The matter is not so simple as that. There were serious faults in great-grandfather's view of the Bible. Sometimes he thought of the Old Testament characters as types of Christ, in such a way that he scarcely saw them as real people. Sometimes, on the other hand, he forgot the difference between the Old Testament and the New, and his Christianity became a religion of a strict way of life governed by rigid rules; the stories were treated as moral examples. Usually he thought that the Creation-story in Genesis must be literally true, because the Bible was the Book of God; therefore the universe was created and made in six days of twenty-four hours each, and all the other statements in the Bible had got to be 'literally' true in the same way.

Hence it was in some ways a healthy reaction when grandfather flung right off and became 'higher critical'.

He saw that the Bible was a book about real men, was written by human authors, and must be studied by the methods of scientific history. He discovered that the folk-lore of other ancient nations showed remarkable likenesses to the Bible stories of the Garden of Eden, the Flood, and the Tower of Babel; hence in studying the Old Testament he could not leave Babylonian mythology out of sight. He came to think of the Old Testament as the story of the development of a warlike Semitic tribe from primitive savagery to something like a decent level of morality and religion. It was evidently a human book; but could it any longer be regarded as the word of God and as 'inspired'? His answer usually was that the 'best' parts of the Old Testament were certainly inspired, but that there were 'degrees of inspiration'; some other parts of it were unedifying, and for religious purposes had better be left unread.

Father, therefore (that is, those of my own generation), usually left them unread, and left the edifying parts unread too; and so did his son and daughter. But in our day some are coming back to rediscover the Old Testament, and begin to see again the things that great-grandfather saw in it.

But it will be inexcusable if they fall into great-grandfather's errors; for he got some things seriously wrong, and grandfather was quite right in applying to the Bible the methods of scientific study. He would indeed have shown small respect for the Bible, if he had shrunk from applying them for fear that it would not stand up to them. He was right about the myths, in a way; but he looked at them rather like an anatomist dissecting specimens, and sometimes he forgot that he, too, was a man, and that the primitive tales at the beginning of Genesis had something to teach *him*.

In truth they had very much to teach him, and you and me also. I want, therefore, to take a look at the old story of Adam and Eve, which is so often ridiculed as not being 'literally' true. But then, what is the writer of it trying to say to us? The fact that *Adam* is simply the Hebrew for 'man' suggests that he intends to tell us a tale about Everyman. Let us see if the story will allow itself to be so treated.

'The Lord God took the Man, and put him into the Garden of Eden to dress it and to keep it' (Gen. ii. 15). And so it is; Man is here in the world to till the soil, provide himself with houses and the other needs of life, get the coal, make machines, build up a civilization. For in God's world he may do what he likes, go where he will, and use the things in the world as he thinks fit; only, he is subject to a prohibition, for he knows that there are some things he may not do. 'Of every tree of the Garden thou mayest freely eat; but of the tree of the knowledge of good and evil, thou shalt not eat of it; for in the day that thou eatest thereof thou shalt surely die' (ii. 16–17).

The story goes on to say that Man needs companionship, 'a help meet for him' (ii. 18). The animals are with us in the world, and we have given them their names, horse, dog, and the rest; but they cannot be in the real sense friends (ii. 18–20). So the Lord God forms the Woman, and brings her to the Man, who at once recognizes her as the 'help' which he needs, and, more than that, as the missing half of himself. He breaks out into the primal love-song (ii. 23):

> This is now bone of my bones,
> And flesh of my flesh;
> She shall be called Woman,
> Because she was taken out of Man.

Such is our original and proper condition: that Man and Woman should live in God's world, together with the animals, using the things in it, and receiving it all as God's gift and obeying His law. But such is not the condition of our life as we know it. Something else has happened.

Where the Serpent came from and how it began to be wicked, we are not told; the story does not go into that, but simply assumes the Serpent's existence, starting from the fact of experience, that we all know how we, living in the world, are liable to be beguiled into doing wrong. The Serpent, then, asks the Woman what God's commandment is, and she tells it (iii. 1–3). It replies that it is not true that in the day that they eat of the forbidden tree they will die (iii. 4). This sounds plausible, and it turns out to be in a sense true, for the Man and Woman go on living for a long time after they have broken God's commandment. It follows from this that when the writer of the story told us in ii. 17 that God attached the penalty of immediate death to the transgression of His commandment, he did not intend that to mean merely physical death, but something more. And so it is. When the Man and the Woman sin, their physical life goes on. But something has died in them: their true manhood. They are no longer the Man and the Woman that God created them to be. We see this in iii. 12; after the Fall, the Man has forgotten all that he had said about the Woman being the other half of himself; she has now become to him 'the Woman whom Thou gavest to be with me', that is, another individual, with whom he must get on as best he can.

What, then, was the Fall? The Serpent said to them that if they were to break God's law, they would be 'as God, knowing good and evil' (iii. 5). Let them refuse to live in subjection to God; let them no longer be content to live as in His world, giving thanks to Him for everything; let them strike out for themselves, and insist on growing up in their own way and doing what they please. That is how Man lives in the world now, forgetting God, seizing greedily on His gifts, grabbing at comforts, pleasures, and advantages, that he may get as much of these as he can in the shortest time, wanting to be independent. Is it not so? Do we not see it in others, and know it in ourselves? Even we who believe that we are in God's world and that all that we have and enjoy is His gift, yet are to be found grabbing at the good things of the world for ourselves without a word of thanks to Him, the Giver.

So, the story continues, work becomes drudgery, and childbirth full of sorrow, and the Man and the Woman have to be turned out of God's Garden (iii. 16–24). A little later on we read, 'The earth was filled with violence; for all flesh had corrupted its way upon the earth' (vi. 12). And that, most unhappily, is the fact; if you would prove it, look at this morning's paper, or into your own heart.

What, then, did the Lord God do about it? The answer to this question occupies all the rest of the Bible.

First, we are told, God commanded a man called Abraham to leave his home and go to a far country (Gen. xii. 1); 'and he went out, not knowing whither he went' (Heb. xi. 8). It was still a dark and sinful world—'the men of Sodom were wicked and sinners before the Lord exceedingly' (Gen. xiii. 13)—but henceforth there were always to be in it some who believed in God and set themselves to obey Him. Abraham is the ancestor of the Israelite nation. We have the tales about Isaac and Jacob and Joseph; but the main story of the Bible begins when the Israelite nation comes into being. It is at this point that we begin to leave myth and pre-historic legend behind, and the narrative to have a firm basis in history.

The Israelites, who had been in servitude in Egypt, had an extraordinary deliverance from that country, and escaped into the desert to the east. They told how the

Lord God had delivered them with a mighty hand and an outstretched arm, and how at Sinai or Horeb He made a Covenant with them, that they should be His people, and He their God. He chose them, not they Him.

His choice of them was not favouritism. He did not destine them to be a master race or *Herrenvolk* (as the Germans believed about themselves when Hitler put across them the Germanic myth), but rather to obey and to suffer, and to learn the elementary lessons about God and the way of His spiritual service, in trust for us and all mankind. For the promise to Abraham was, according to the text from Genesis which St. Paul quotes in Galatians iii. 8, that in his seed all the nations of the world should be blessed.

The discipline through which God put His chosen nation included that of defeat, complete political ruin, and deportation to Babylon, at the Fall of Jerusalem in 586 B.C. But because through all this they still believed that God was in control of all that was happening, and accepted their sufferings as His punishment for their sins, they were able to be told of His purpose of the future: there would be a Second Exodus (Jer. xxiii. 7–8), a New Covenant (Jer. xxxi. 31–4), an outpouring on them of God's Holy Spirit, that they might see visions and dream dreams (Joel ii. 28), but above all that they might obey His will (Ezekiel xxxvi. 26–7). Finally, all nations were to come and share in these blessings (Isaiah xlv. 20–3).

The message of the New Testament is simply that all this has happened. Jesus is the Christ, that is, the Messiah or Anointed One, the King to whose coming the prophets looked forward. Hence without the New Testament the Old Testament is incomplete. But without the Old Testament we could not begin to understand what the New Testament is telling us.

A. G. HEBERT, S.S.M.

Where the Four Gospels don't Agree, Which One are We to Believe?

BEHIND this question lies a deeper question: Why are there four gospels at all? In reality there is only one Gospel, that is, one revelation of God through the Lord Jesus Christ; indeed the title for each of these four books was 'The Gospel according to So-and-so'. Why then did the Church keep four? Would not one record of the Gospel have been sufficient, say, that of Luke, who claims to have studied his many predecessors? Our four, and our four alone, were retained because it was believed that they were either written or inspired by apostles of the Lord Jesus; thus even Mark was not dropped, although most of it had been embodied in Matthew and Luke, since it was supposed to incorporate reminiscences of Peter. While the common title of the books was 'The Gospel', or good news, to each was added 'according to Matthew, Mark, &c.', as the case might be, the idea being to stress the common message and the unity of faith in all four, despite their varieties and idiosyncrasies. But even so difficulties were soon felt, such as we feel to-day, owing to the juxtaposition of treatises which had originally circulated in separate circles of the Church. Christians who noticed the repetitions, the more or less serious discrepancies, and the omissions, endeavoured to solve such perplexities in various ways, none of which was more notable than the effort of a Syrian scholar called Tatian, in the second century, to compile a harmony or single Gospel, which actually was used by the Syrian Church, in preference to the four, for over two centuries. When people had such a smooth fusion of the gospel stories, they were obviously freed from any of the embarrassing difficulties which to-day start the question,

'Where the four gospels differ, which are we to believe?'
As we cannot take Tatian's short cut, we have to answer
that question as best we may.

One or two general principles of literary and historical
criticism must be borne in mind, if the answer is to be
rightly sought.

(*a*) You cannot answer it simply by counting heads,
three or two against one. This is no case of four independent witnesses, as used to be thought. Thus Mark (and I
use these four names for the sake of convenience in referring to the four) was known to Matthew and to Luke—
that is, Mark practically as we have it. John was familiar
with some of the traditions incorporated in the other and
earlier three, even if he did not know any or all of them.
Hence, what occurs in two or more may really go back
to one.

(*b*) Neither can you appeal to one gospel invariably
against or above the other three. Though Mark was the
earliest, this does not imply that it covered all the ground.
Rich traditions about Jesus were current in the primitive
Church, which were not accessible to the writer or which
he passed over as irrelevant to his particular purpose;
because they only occur in a later narrative, this does
not necessarily prove that they were less authentic or
reliable. A touch or tradition may not be inferior simply
because it is preserved in a source outside Mark. While
Mark underlies the others, it did not reap the entire field;
thus we cannot infer that because something occurs in
Mark alone, it is therefore superior in value to material
harvested in one or more of the other three.

(*c*) Again, the omission of a story or saying in one
gospel does not prove in every case that the writer disbelieved it. For books in the ancient world were limited
in size; if a writer did not require certain material for his
own interpretation, he might leave it out in order to
make room for fresh data. Thus Luke in all likelihood

omitted, for want of space, one entire section of Mark
(vi. 45–viii. 26).

(d) On the other hand, Mark frequently does preserve
a version which is not so much affected by later tradition.
In deciding which account is preferable, at any given
point, we may safely assign the Marcan version more
weight, since it gives a more original reflection of what
was actually said or done; it seems often to be more naïve,
less conscious of literary and religious purpose than the
other three, and therefore it may be held to represent
more accurately upon the whole the content of the primitive testimony.

Such considerations hint that there is no rough-and-
ready method of arranging the four gospels in order of
merit, for our purpose. They are all more or less books
made out of books; behind them lie literary sources
already used by different circles in the Church, which
were drawn up as well as used by preachers or teachers.
More than that, behind and around even these sources
lay the oral tradition, in which nothing was committed to
writing. Now the Oriental memory was extraordinarily
retentive, but, under the breath of a fresh faith, it could be
imaginative, and traditions were shaped, embroidered,
and recast for the purposes of edification. Stories might
be amplified, heightened, and idealized in the light of
faith. Besides, every writer of a gospel had his own
interests. None set out to be an impartial biographer of
Jesus. Not that this makes them less trustworthy, for any
record of history has a purpose behind it; stories have
generally a case to represent; the presence of a motive or
of motives does not necessarily invalidate the account, it
merely suggests the line to be taken in weighing what is
recorded, especially when this can be compared with
another version. Luke's sympathies, aims, and interests
were not quite the same as those of Matthew, for instance.
In each case, the writer told his story, selecting the

material, arranging it, and shaping it for his special purpose. It is only by appreciating such prepossessions and characteristics, as well as the unconscious prepossessions of faith with a story to tell, that we moderns can arrive at a balance between the various traditions lying in our four gospels.

The bearing of these general principles may best be shown by applying them to definite cases. Take one or two concrete illustrations.

(i) When did Jesus purge the temple in Jerusalem? John says, at the beginning of his ministry; the other three put it at the end. Good scholars have made out a case for John's dating, which deserves consideration. However this may be, it illustrates (*a*); the point is that you cannot decide simply by counting three against one, you must weigh the likelihood of one or the other tradition being a deliberate alteration of the other, and ask, in the light of internal evidence, which? This evidence is the general character of the gospel or gospels in question.

(ii) Again, when were the first disciples called by Jesus? Mark and Matthew put this, as an abrupt summons, in Galilee; John suggests that Jesus had already met the four disciples at the revival mission of John the Baptist in Judea. It is not impossible that John's tradition preserves an historical truth, since psychologically it explains the apparently sudden call to the apostleship later on. This illustrates (*b*), for it is likely that Jesus did more work in Judea than any evangelist realized till John.

(iii) When did Jesus utter parables like the Grain of Mustard-seed and the Woman with the Leaven? Matthew inserts them in a long address, among other parables; Luke makes Jesus tell these two stories (which we call parables) in a moment of enthusiasm, after his healing of a crippled woman had impressed the crowd

(xiii. 10–20). The latter setting is more likely. It is not that we can hope to ascertain the precise time and place at which Jesus said certain words; and, like a true teacher, he would often repeat his sayings. But Matthew, with catechetical interests, liked to group sayings in large sections which, we may be reasonably sure, are artificial, whereas the more natural occasion seems in this particular case to be that indicated by Luke. Why Mark omitted the second and John both of these stories is indicated in (b) and (c); John indeed has no parables such as the other three record.

Finally (iv) the truth of (d) is shown by the answer of Jesus to the disciples when they wondered why he did not stay at Capernaum. Mark makes him explain that he had a wider mission throughout the country (i. 37, 38); Luke (iv. 42, 43) thinks it was because he had been 'sent' from heaven—a true, and a deep, explanation, but plainly less appropriate in this connexion. Again, in the parable of the wicked vinedressers, Mark tells naturally how they murdered the owner's son and then flung him outside the vineyard; Matthew and Luke, impressed by the details of the crucifixion which took place outside the city, make the vinedressers throw the son outside first and then kill him. The preference in a case like this clearly is in favour of Mark.

These illustrations may serve to indicate how careful we have to be in weighing the evidence before we answer our question. There is no rigid rule. Which gospel we are to believe depends at any point upon a comparative judgement of several. Especially in considering discrepancies within the narratives of the crucifixion and the appearances after death, we ought to appreciate the creative as well as the reproductive tendencies of the writers, the ethos of each gospel, and the connexion between them, if any. How far was one correcting the other? How far was one developing a theme of his own, independently? Each gospel, even that of Mark, has its particular interests, its way of putting things, its reason for representing certain facts, or what seem to be facts, thus and not otherwise. All this does not necessarily mean that the testimony is lowered in value, as I have already hinted. Luke's interest in prayer and in women, for instance, might make him more specially alive to preserve stories and sayings about such matters; it need not follow that he invented them, any more than Matthew did in bringing out the prophetic opposition of Jesus to the Jewish authorities, which did not happen to appeal so much to Luke. The point is, that we must take these and other factors into account as we decide between one line or item of tradition and another.

Such a process of examination may seem round-about and hesitating, but it is only by this patient, frank, searching study of the records in their divergencies that one can reach an appreciation of the common faith which they attest. The four gospels turn out to be records, not only of the faith which they imply but of the Person who evoked that faith. Sometimes we cannot be sure how this or that happened; but as a rule we realize that something did happen, even though it is not told in ways that convince us as they convinced the earliest readers, that something was said, even though it has come down in different versions. The more thorough, unprejudiced, and honest we are in facing the differences, major and minor, the more likely we are to be sensible that underneath them there is an historical basis sufficient for faith. In other words, if we ask, why are there differences in the four gospels? the answer is not that each of them is representing a different Jesus, but that it is the same Jesus; only, the truth about Him did not pass fully into any one of them, and it is part of our discipline to use them, with perfectly candid minds, in order to see Him for ourselves as these early writers saw His reality for themselves and for their age. In practising this study, most people discover that when the four gospels differ, they are not driven to disbelieve all of them, but to find that in one or another there is trustworthy evidence for a reasonable faith.

JAMES MOFFATT

Can we Believe all the things we read of in the New Testament?

YOU want to know whether the things about which you read in the New Testament are really true. I am not surprised that you should raise this question. For of course the New Testament is the most important book in the world; and the story which it has to tell us about Jesus Christ and his followers is the most important story in the world. Naturally both the book and the story would at once lose their importance for us if we had any reason to think that they dealt with things which never really happened.

1. Now the first thing I want to assure you is that the people about whom you read in the New Testament were real people. You may take it for granted (no reliable student of the New Testament doubts this) that nineteen hundred years ago Jesus went about preaching and teaching in Galilee and Judea, and that after a brief ministry His enemies secured His condemnation before the Roman Governor, Pontius Pilate, and had Him put to death by crucifixion. This is vouched for even by a famous Roman historian, Tacitus, who writes: 'Christ, from whom the Christians received their name, had during the Emperorship of Tiberius been condemned and punished by Pontius Pilate.' There is also no doubt that during His ministry Jesus had gathered around Him a band of loyal, earnest, and teachable disciples, who came to recognize, even during His lifetime, that He was no ordinary preacher and teacher, but was (they said) 'the Christ, the Son of the Living God'. And being convinced, in a way that left no room for doubt, that after His crucifixion He had been raised by God from the dead, these disciples

and others who became attached to their fellowship began to testify about Him 'in Jerusalem, and in all Judæa, and in Samaria, and unto the uttermost part of the earth',[1] proclaiming that He was the Messiah by whom God was offering salvation to men, and was ultimately to establish His Kingdom. Among these early followers was an ardent young Jew, Saul (or Paul) of Tarsus, who after being for a time a bitter opponent and persecutor, was supernaturally converted, and thereafter laboured incessantly to carry the Gospel of Jesus throughout the length and breadth of the then known world. Most people who really know what he accomplished would include St. Paul among the ten greatest men in the history of the world; and if you want to know his story you will find reliable evidence, firstly in those remarkable Epistles which he himself wrote, and secondly in the book of Acts, written by his travel-companion, St. Luke. Let me add here that the Epistles of St. Paul were written within from twenty to thirty years after the crucifixion of Jesus. Is that not in itself a good guarantee that the wonderful things which he has to declare about Jesus had a sure basis in historical fact?

It is worth while to recall that, just as the people mentioned in the New Testament were real, so too, of course, were the places. Some day you may visit Bethlehem, where Jesus was born; Nazareth, where He was brought up; Capernaum (now in ruins, as He declared would be the case), where He did so many of His wonderful works; Jerusalem, where He was condemned to die; and similarly you may be able to visit the ancient cities to which St. Paul and his fellow apostles carried the Gospel.

2. I should like also to assure you that the stories in the New Testament were written by people who had

[1] Acts i. 8.

good knowledge of the things they were writing about. It used to be alleged in some quarters that the book of Acts was quite unreliable as history. But to-day the prevailing opinion among scholars is that Acts is on the whole a carefully composed and trustworthy document; and Sir William Ramsay, one of the foremost of modern authorities on ancient history, has even declared that its author is to be placed 'among the historians of the first rank'. An interesting fact is that in various parts of his narrative, for instance, in chapter xxvii, the writer uses the first personal pronoun ('*we* sailed', '*we* came', &c.); and from this it may be inferred that he was himself present on these occasions.

Similarly, we have good reason to trust the accounts of Jesus' public ministry given in the Gospels. It has for long been a widely accepted opinion that the earliest of the four Gospels, that of St. Mark, was not written before A.D. 65, and the latest of them, that of St. John, not before A.D. 90; but now there is a growing tendency among scholars to assign them all to earlier dates, or at least to recognize that there must have been other documents of an earlier date from which our present Gospels have been composed. The Gospels are all based on the reminiscences of people who had known Jesus in the flesh, who had heard Him preaching and telling his unforgettable parables, who had seen His tender sympathy with those who were in suffering or need, His forbearing and forgiving attitude towards His accusers, His unflinching courage in face of opposition, danger, and death. And these people tell what they remember about Him for the simple reason that, like St. Peter before the Sanhedrin, they 'cannot but speak the things which they have seen and heard'.

All this makes it plain that the New Testament narratives are in a very different category from the legendary stories which have grown up around the

name of Buddha and other great religious teachers of
the ancient world. In saying this I do not forget that
legends did grow up in course of time around the names
of Jesus and His disciples. There are many legends in
the 'apocryphal' Gospels—Gospels, that is, which the
Church refused to recognize and which are therefore
not included in the New Testament. Thus in the so-
called 'Gospel according to Thomas' we read how the
boy Jesus when five years old made twelve sparrows
out of clay; then He clapped His hands and they all
flew off! The fantastic character of some of the stories
in the apocryphal Gospels helps by contrast to show
how very much more reliable are the stories in the New
Testament.

3. It does not follow, however, that everything in
the New Testament is to be accepted without question
as accurate history. It is well in this connexion to
remind ourselves how the four Gospels came to be
written. While the authors never wrote down anything
but what they believed to be true, their aim in writing
was not to provide readers in the twentieth century
with a detailed and accurate history-book concerning
Jesus and His followers. If that had been their aim,
we may be sure they would have included much that
has been omitted, and made clear much that has been
left obscure. The fact rather is that they wrote as men
who had come to believe in Jesus; and in the Gospels
they have preserved, without any pretence at complete-
ness, various stories and sayings which might help
other people to see in Him 'the Christ, the Son of God'.[1]

This being the case, we cannot rule out altogether
the possibility that in some instances their beliefs may
have come to colour their narratives, and that the
original facts may in certain particulars have been
rather different from the stories which grew up around

[1] John xx. 30. 31.

them. Take, for example, the strange story of how with five loaves and two fishes Jesus miraculously fed a crowd of five thousand people. Can it be, as has been suggested, that what really took place was that Jesus invited the crowd to participate in a 'sacramental' act, and that the idea that 'they were all filled' is based on a misconception? Similarly, to take an example from the book of Acts, where it is said that after the Pentecost experience the followers of Jesus began to speak with tongues. We know that generally 'to speak with tongues' means to be carried away into unintelligible outbursts of praise or prayer, and it is possible that the writer here is in error in representing the disciples as speaking intelligibly in various languages. But when all allowance has been made in such-like cases for the possibility of misunderstanding, it nevertheless remains true that the New Testament narratives, taken as a whole, are a reliable account of events which really happened.

4. There is one other thing to be kept in mind when we ask how far the New Testament stories are true. A thing may not be *literally* true, and yet be true in a deeper and far more important sense; and this is especially the case where religious truth is concerned. Much of the extraordinary imagery in the book of Revelation, for instance, is an attempt to portray in picture-language the eternal warfare between good and evil, or, as we may say, between God and the Devil; and some of the details in the picture, like the appearance of the Beast which men are forced to worship, have special reference to the persecution of Christians under the Roman Empire, and are not without parallel in the history of Europe to-day. So, too, when we read in other parts of the New Testament of angels bringing spoken messages to men, of the Devil appearing to tempt Jesus, of Heaven as a place of blessedness apparently above the skies, and of Hell as a place of

torment with unquenchable fire, we must recognize that we are dealing with attempts to describe religious truth by means of word-pictures, and it is stupid to interpret them as if they were literal fact.

5. Other contributors to this series have set themselves to answer your questions regarding the miracles of Jesus, and the stories of His Birth and Resurrection; so I shall content myself with only a few words with regard to these topics.

(a) The miracles of Jesus. It is quite possible, as I have suggested above, that the original facts about some of the miracles of Jesus may have been different from some of the stories which have come down to us; for when people are filled with wonder at something which has happened in their midst they sometimes misunderstand its true significance. But that Jesus did work miracles, or 'works of power' as the Gospels prefer to call them, is a fact we ought not for a moment to doubt. Filled as He was with an unconquerable faith in God His Father, He was ready when occasion arose to manifest His faith in action.

(b) The Virgin Birth and the Resurrection of Jesus. There are stories in the New Testament which clearly imply (i) that Jesus was miraculously born of the Virgin Mary without a human father, and (ii) that after having been dead for two days He began to appear in some sort of bodily form to His followers and that His grave was found empty. Despite the obvious difficulty of these stories, there are strong reasons why we should accept them as having a real basis in fact. If you feel that you cannot be sure about them, I would ask you at least to keep an open mind, for the evidence in their favour is too strong to be rejected off-hand.

Whatever difficulties you may have about some of the stories of Jesus, remember that the New Testament bears witness from first to last that Jesus was no ordinary man, but was, as we say, God revealed in human form, One who in His human life manifested the holiness and love and power which we associate with God Himself. It is this fact, and not merely the story of His birth, which Christians have in mind when they declare that Jesus is 'the Son of God'; and it is this fact, taken in conjunction with the other evidence for His resurrection, which has made Christians in all ages believe with conviction that He is alive for ever more and is the conquercr over sin and death. You will never quite understand the New Testament so long as you are content to think of Jesus as merely one of the world's great heroes, like Socrates or Buddha or Julius Caesar; but once you see that in Him God has done something quite unique for the world, sending, as we say, His own Son to accomplish the world's salvation, then the New Testament will become the most wonderful book in the world for you; and you will feel it to be all the more wonderful because you will know it to be true.

GEORGE S. DUNCAN

Did not St. Paul spoil the Simple Religion of Jesus?

THE criticism is frequently made that Paul was responsible for changing the whole character of Christianity. His Christ, it is said, is a totally different figure from the Jesus of the Evangelists, his gospel far removed from the simplicities of Galilee. He has led the Church along a track which its own Founder never intended. He has turned the stream of Christianity out of the channel which Jesus made for it. He has almost entirely ignored the facts of Jesus' earthly ministry. He has actually disclaimed interest in 'Christ after the flesh'.[1] He tells us frankly that his gospel is something completely independent: he positively glories in its independence.[2] In fact, Christianity as we know it to-day has had two founders, not one. Jesus indeed led the way. He came heralding the kingdom of heaven and the Fatherhood of God, bidding all men repent and believe and accept the forgiveness of their sins: and 'the common people heard Him gladly'.[3] But when this gracious message had passed through the hands and the brain of the ex-disciple of Gamaliel, when the good news of Christ had been subjected to the tortuous thought-processes and speculations of the converted Pharisee, what emerged was something so different that it was barely recognizable. Religion had become theology. Jesus' offer of free salvation had become an intricate theory of justification. 'The wondrous cross on which the Prince of glory died' had become a dogma of atonement. All manner of complexities of doctrine, unwarranted in their origin and ruinous in their effect, have been Paul's legacy to the Church. If you would recapture the pure, undefiled

[1] 2 Cor. v. 16.   [2] Gal. i. 11 f.   [3] Mark xii. 27.

Gospel, it is said, you must first eliminate the Pauline elements. 'Back from Paul to Jesus', is the cry.

This criticism of the great New Testament apostle looks formidable. But, in point of fact, it is off the track completely.

To set Paul over against Jesus, as a second 'founder' of Christianity, or as the arch-corrupter of the authentic Gospel, betokens a lamentably superficial and defective understanding alike of the 'simplicities of Galilee' and of the great central themes of the epistles. The alleged twist Paul gave to the original message, turning it into something quite different, is really a myth.

What are the facts?

Certainly Paul claims independence for his gospel. '*My* gospel', he is never tired of calling it. And certainly his was one of the most creative minds the Church has ever known. A dull, unimaginative borrower he could never be. He had far too much of the passion of the explorer to plagiarize his creed from Peter or James or any one else. But does that mean disloyalty to Christ? Surely all living religion must strike the independent, original note. There is no vital gospel into which the personal equation does not enter. And Paul's religion was true to Jesus precisely in the degree in which it was emphatically his own.

But why, it is asked, are the references in the epistles to the life and character and teaching of Jesus so meagre? Part of the answer is that these references, as any careful study will show, are not nearly so few and scarce as is commonly supposed. The other part of the answer lies in the fact—so often strangely overlooked—that in the epistles Paul is not preaching to the unconverted who had never heard of Jesus, but addressing his Christian brethren who were in vital, daily fellowship with the living and exalted Christ. For them, Jesus had passed for ever beyond the limitations which had bound Him while He remained a physical presence with His first disciples, roaming with them through the cornfields and the vineyards, and keeping vigil at night beneath the Syrian sky. He was nearer now than He had ever been in those days of Galilee, nearer even than when Peter and Andrew had rowed Him in their boat across the highland loch, nearer than when Mary of Bethany had welcomed Him to her home and sat at His feet listening to His words. He was more than a memory, more than a historic example: He was a present possession, and His friendship the most intimate reality of life.

This does not mean that Paul was indifferent to the historic facts. It does not mean that he proclaimed salvation through the death and resurrection of a vague 'God-Man' whom no one really knew. On the contrary: the saving efficacy of that death and resurrection was due precisely to this—that it was *Jesus* who had died and risen again; and when Paul had access to and communion with God the Father, it was through One who still wore the lineaments of Him who was 'made of a woman, made under the law',[1] who was 'meek and gentle',[2] 'patient',[3] 'humble', 'obedient unto death, even the death of the cross', One who had travelled that earthly road to His final exaltation.[4] The story of the Master's life and character never ceased to be treasured. 'Can we have any doubt', writes Professor John Baillie, referring to the wonderful picture of Christian character in 1 Corinthians xiii, 'who it was who sat in the studio of Paul's imagination for that famous little vignette of the ideal man?'[5]

Again, take Paul's teaching on justification. This is the point at which his accusers grow loudest and most positive in their criticism. Here, it is said, is a flagrant instance of the apostle's habit of corrupting the simple

[1] Gal. iv. 4.   [2] 2 Cor. x. 1.   [3] Thess. iii. 5.   [4] Phil. ii. 8–11.
[5] *The Place of Jesus Christ in Modern Christianity*, p. 81.

Gospel by the introduction of alien ideas; and Christianity has never quite recovered from the damage thus inflicted upon it.

If this criticism were sound, it would be hard to understand why the doctrine of a God who 'justifieth the ungodly'[1] should have remained so fruitful throughout the centuries. How many of the historic revivals of religion have sprung from a rediscovery of this great article of faith! Too often have pedantic commentators, lacking Paul's tremendous encounter with Christ, and having no real kinship with his inner experience, overlaid this doctrine with the verbiage of a dreary scholasticism, and darkened counsel by words without knowledge. But to any one who has some spiritual sympathy with the apostle, and some understanding of what it means to owe everything in life to God's sheer unmerited grace, it is apparent that Paul is here unfolding the central truths of Jesus' message. For what does justification mean? It means that no man can save himself, and that salvation is of the Lord. It means that all ideas of human merit are excluded. It means that in the work of reconciliation God—not man—holds the initiative. What is this but the very core of the teaching of Jesus? It is a making explicit of what lies implicit in the parables of the labourers in the vineyard, the Pharisee and the publican, the younger son and the elder brother, and many another. It is not only true to the Master's teachings, but true also to His whole attitude to sinners, when He sought them out and took the first step to end the alienation, true above all to the cross where He died to break the last barriers down. Jesus was the initiative of God incarnate. He was the bridge thrust out—from God's side—across the estranging gulf. He was the divine promise of a new career to men and women who had bungled life hopelessly and settled down into despair.

[1] Rom. iv. 5.

Paul's thought of justification was no theological speculation: it was the focus of an intensely evangelical experience. It contains the very kernel of the Gospel which
Jesus lived and died to bring.

Hence the charge that Paul changed the whole character of Christianity is quite without foundation. So far
from being the arch-corrupter of the faith, he was its
chief defender. To him, more than to any other before
or since, it was given to draw those tremendous conclusions—the eternal Sonship, the all-sufficiency of grace,
the invincible determination of God to 'sum up all things
in Christ'[1]—to which the life and death and resurrection of his Lord had pointed. 'Life means Christ to me',
he once said:[2] and generations yet unborn will bless him
for interpreting Christ so faithfully, and for making the
road to God through Christ so very clear and plain.

JAMES S. STEWART

[1] Eph. i. 10.   [2] Phil. i. 21 (Moffatt).

What became of the Apostles? Why do we hear so little about them?

THE question has been asked: Why do we hear so little about the disciples or the apostles? Well, in order to answer that we have to ask two other questions: first, who the apostles were, and next, what do we actually hear about them either in the New Testament or outside it? Now in the first three Gospels we do not hear a great deal: we are told that Jesus called four of them—Simon (or Peter) and Andrew, James and John, two pairs of brothers—while they were fishing, and another, Matthew (or Levi), when he was sitting at the receipt of custom. Then we learn that He took Peter, James, and John with Him when He raised Jairus's daughter and when He was transfigured: we hear of some occasions when Peter took the lead in asking Him questions; and we also hear that He chose twelve men, that is, seven more besides those whom He had specially called. These were Philip, Bartholomew, Thomas, another James, another Simon called Zelotes, a Judas otherwise called Thaddaeus, and Judas Iscariot. So much for the first three Gospels. In the fourth, we have a little more; we find one Nathaniel, who is generally thought to be the same as Bartholomew, being called by Jesus; we also have certain of them speaking, namely, Philip, Andrew, Judas who was not Iscariot; and we hear a good deal about Thomas. We also know from *all* the Gospels that Judas Iscariot was the betrayer. So in the four Gospels all of them make some appearance except two—Simon Zelotes and James the son of Alphaeus. Then in the Acts we have a list of the same names as in Luke—naturally, since he wrote both Gospel and Acts. We hear of the bad end of Judas Iscariot and how he was replaced by Matthias; and on that occasion we are told the name of another who had been a personal disciple of Jesus, namely Joseph who was called Barsabas and surnamed Justus. Later on we find that James the brother of John was beheaded by Herod. Philip, too, we hear about: but he was not one of the twelve, but one of the seven deacons who were appointed along with Stephen; and we cannot be sure (though it is likely enough) that some or all of those seven had been among Jesus' disciples; like others who are mentioned here and there, particularly Mnason, who is described as 'an old disciple'.

But when we have collected all we can out of the New Testament, the fact still remains that we do know very little about most of the twelve apostles, and naturally even less about the seventy disciples. What is the reason of this? I believe the principal one is, not that they did not amply deserve to be remembered, but that all the books, if there were any, which recorded anything about their later lives and deaths are lost. Outside the books which make up the New Testament, there are hardly any Christian writings dating between the years 100 and 150. Moreover, we only know of two writers of that period who wrote down any recollections of the early days: one was called Papias (about 130) and the other Hegesippus (about 150): and of their books we only have a few quotations, picked out, most of them, by the man who, in the fourth century, wrote the first great history of the Church, namely Eusebius. Papias tells a little about Matthew and John and Mark, and mentions a disciple called Aristion: Hegesippus gives the story of the death of James the brother of the Lord, and speaks of some descendants of Jude. We would give anything to have the whole of the books which these two men wrote, for though Eusebius preserved what he thought were their most interesting statements, we may be sure that there was a great deal more, which seemed to him so familiar as not to be worth quoting, but which has since been forgotten: just as nowadays we find it very difficult to make out exactly how our parents and grandparents behaved and dressed, and so on; and just as we think we can never be in danger of forgetting what we do ourselves, but all the same we do forget it as time goes on.

Then we have to remember that the apostles were not chosen by Jesus because they were particularly clever, still less learned men. They were not. In our Lord's life-time Peter took the lead among them; but the questions he asked and the things he said were not clever, rather the reverse. Still, we see that Jesus had great confidence in him, saw that he was in himself a strong character, and called him a Rock; and we see that he grew in knowledge and strength, and was enabled to be still the leader after our Lord had passed out of this world. But, as we read in the Acts, the Jewish authorities found, and were surprised to find, that the apostles were ignorant and illiterate men. Paul, who was not one of them, was in fact the only man in the early days who was possessed of the learning of his time, and was able to write (and write magnificently) in Greek.

What, then, became of the apostles? They had our Lord's commission to preach, to tell every one what they had seen and heard of Him, and especially about His resurrection. And this no doubt they did; but we have no details. There are but one or two ancient traditions which we are justified in believing: that Peter went to Rome is one, and that he was martyred in the persecution under Nero. The later story says that he was crucified head downwards at his own request. That he was crucified is likely enough, and that it was done in mockery of his Master; but that he was crucified head downwards is not at all probable. That John went to Asia Minor— to Ephesus—and ended his life there peacefully as a very old man is also to be believed; before that, he had been banished to Patmos. We have seen too that his brother James was beheaded at a very early date. It is also a very persistent tradition that Thomas went to India. Apart from these, who were of the twelve, we have good authority (that of Josephus and Hegesippus) for saying that James the brother of the Lord, whom we find in the Acts as leader of the Church at Jerusalem, was put to death by the Jews, and that one Simeon succeeded him, who was also called a brother of the Lord, and was eventually crucified in his old age. But neither of them was of the twelve. That very nearly exhausts our knowledge.

There was another thing which was likely enough to confuse the minds of people in after years. This was the fact that several of the twelve, and of the early disciples, bore the same names, and some had, it seems, two names. Thus there were two Jameses in the twelve, and the 'brother of the Lord' besides. There were two Simons, Peter and the Canaanite; there was a Judas besides Judas Iscariot, and yet a third, brother of the Lord and perhaps writer of the Epistle of Jude. Then, again, Matthew seems to have had another name, Levi; Bartholomew 'son of Talmai' was also Nathaniel; Thaddaeus was probably another name for one of the Judases; Philip the apostle and Philip the deacon were two different persons. All this would be difficult to keep in mind in the absence of carefully written records, of which, as we have seen, there are hardly any outside the New Testament. Not that in later days people were content with that. They said that after Pentecost the apostles met and divided the world among them: Andrew went to Greece, Bartholomew to Persia, Thomas, as I said, to India, Matthew to Ethiopia, and so on; and a multitude of legends were written about the wonderful adventures which befell them in all these countries. All of them except John, it was said, suffered martyrdom; and hence it is that the images and pictures of them which you may see in churches represent them as holding crosses or spears or axes. But you cannot place any confidence in these later stories, the oldest of which was not written before about the year 150. In all likelihood a number of the twelve died natural deaths in Palestine and the countries adjoining it; and probably few of them lived to see the destruction of Jerusalem, which took place in the year 70. The great thing about them must have been that, like the Jews in the early days, the people whom they met and lived with 'took knowledge of them that they had been with Jesus'.

MONTAGUE R. JAMES

Shouldn't all Christians be Pacifists?

IN the earliest period of persecution Christians felt themselves under no obligation to assist the secular power of the State in any active way and were in that sense pacifists. As soon as it became possible for Christians to serve in the Roman army a problem arose as to whether such service was compatible with their faith. Ever since, opinion has been divided between those who acknowledge a duty to support legitimate public authority to the extent of fighting for it, or to oppose illegitimate authority to the extent of fighting against it, and those who refuse to take part in any acts of violence.

There is no difficulty about naming the latter; 'pacifist' is the recognized name; there is about the former. 'Anti-pacifist' is wrong because they are supporting not opposing, 'militarist' is unfair. Perhaps I might be allowed to call them 'just-belligerent', in spite of, or because of the pun. Official Christian approval of war has always been conditional on its being considered a just war, justly fought; and the sincere Christian can hardly enter on war except with reluctance. These two attitudes are strictly incompatible, because no compromise is possible; a man must either fight or refuse to fight. The arguments for and against have already been gone through many times and are no more effective than any other arguments on practical issues which divide men sharply. I should have no excuse for saying anything on the subject but that the new developments in warfare, culminating (for the present) in the atomic bomb, have narrowed and to some extent altered the issue between them.

Let us for a moment look at the controversy in a detached way to see what is characteristic of each side.

The pacifist attitude is essentially a protest against something easily forgotten because it is always there; namely, that human political institutions rest in the last resort on violence, on the prison and the gallows. That is not as it ought to be. None can touch pitch without being defiled; evil means corrupt the best conceived ends; as a matter of plain historical fact those who take the sword generally perish by the sword. There is a good deal of reason for the prison and the gallows as instruments of authority within the state, since they do preserve order fairly successfully. There is much less for warfare between states.

On the other hand pacifists are a minority and their protest is possible and valuable as that of a minority and in no other way. If by any chance the majority turned pacifist, that would leave power in the hands of the residue of thugs to be found in any population, the unscrupulous, the violent, the criminal. The state of affairs would be something like that of Nazi Germany. The majority of Germans were not pacifist, but they were non-resisters; they went the way they were led or pushed, and the thugs did what they liked.

Using the figures merely for illustration, let us suppose that the population consists of 2 per cent. pacifists who detest all violence, 2 per cent. thugs who like it, and the rest in between. Of this 96 per cent. those at the top will lean somewhat towards pacifism and those at the bottom towards thuggism. But on the whole it is the anti-thuggism of the vast majority that keeps the thugs down and from them the just-belligerents are recruited. One of the gravest difficulties up to the present has been that most of this 96 per cent., just as they have taken for granted the use of force for keeping the peace within the state, have taken for granted also warfare between states, as something that happens and will always go on happening. During the last few years a great many have been roused to realize that if mankind does not put an end to war, war can put an end to mankind. This is something new.

Gibbon, the historian, writing in the last quarter of the eighteenth century, could assume quite seriously, and not without some reason, that Europeans had so tamed warfare among themselves that it had become relatively harmless, a sport of kings; and that Europeans were so superior in military technique that they had nothing to fear from outside. The Napoleonic wars should have upset that complacency a bit. Nearly every war since has gone farther in the way of indiscriminate slaughter and destruction. Few, perhaps, have been so complacent as Gibbon, but on the whole the attitude of the just-belligerent has been that war is an ailment—a chronic one and not too severe. The pacifists have taken rather the same view because they have been content to live in and co-operate with a society which took war for granted, frequently indulged in it and was always preparing for it. Both acquiesced, though they acquiesced in a different way. It is at this point that the issue has changed and both parties may be changing their minds.

The change has come about through a change in military technique which Gibbon could not foresee. In the old days of weapons of limited range and power, it was possible to distinguish between combatant and non-combatant and keep the process of slaughter and destruction within definite bounds; in short, you could fight a battle in one field while the ploughman was at work in the next. As the means available were feeble so also the ends were limited. On the whole, defence was stronger than offence. (The exceptions have been where one side was technically superior; but no people with energy and intelligence had need to be inferior in technique for long.) Thus would-be aggressors had only limited expectations. However greedy and unscrupulous they were by nature, reason acted as a check on their ambitions. Few combatants have ever entered a war with complete justice on their side, and probably none, during the course of operations, have kept entirely within the bounds of just action; but in the past injustice could be and sometimes was kept within bounds.

That cannot be said now. The war of 1914–18 produced more slaughter and destruction less discriminately than any previous war. In the war of 1939–45 indiscriminate slaughter and destruction attained a climax that nobody could even have imagined beforehand. In no war have the aggressors more clearly betrayed themselves than did Hitler in a whole series of acts from 1938 to 1941 and Japan in 1941; so that the Allies entered the war with cleaner hands than most combatants in most wars. That did not prevent them from using means of indiscriminate attack on whole populations, which few would have approved of beforehand in cold blood. It is fantastic to suppose that once a war has started any combatant possessing a weapon as decisive as the atomic bomb would refrain from using it. There may have been wars in which those who had what they considered a decisive weapon refrained from using it, but they are certainly exceptions, and there is no reason to suppose that the next war, if there is one, would be an exception. Another war between Great Powers is likely to exceed the war of 1939–45 in horrors, as much as it exceeded the First World War. To say it would destroy civilization is probably an exaggeration, but it would certainly be a disaster such as nobody but a devil would wish to bring about. Even the 2 per cent. of thugs, who are still human, might recoil from the prospect, although the anarchy that follows wholesale destruction gives the surviving thugs brief but glorious opportunities.

There can hardly be security against another war until national armies and armaments are reduced to the modest level required for police purposes, by means of a world authority with powers overriding existing national sovereignty. To establish such an authority will not be easy and will take a long time. There are wide differences of opinion as to what powers it should possess and by what means it should exercise them. There is likely to be a difficult period after it is nominally established before it can exercise genuine power. Lastly there is nothing in the nature of things to prevent a world authority from becoming oppressive, corrupt or ineffective. Nevertheless the risk must be taken, because the alternative is international anarchy such as exists at present, with only slight mitigation. There is some mitigation because world organizations of sorts are functioning in a precarious fashion. As long as they function at all there is some hope. However, the period of greatest danger is now, before the world authority is set up.

The constructive task of setting up a world authority is work for the statesmen, not for private individuals, private organizations, churches, or even political parties as such. The first moves can only come from those who already possess national authority; only those who exercise existing sovereignty can initiate the surrender of sovereignty. An important beginning can be made by statesmen who are willing to turn matters of international politics into matters of international law by submitting disputes to arbitration. The rest of us who are not statesmen can do little directly except applaud and encourage moves in the right direction and protest against moves in the wrong one.

Indirectly a good deal can be done by discouraging everything that makes for fear and suspicion. Heads of governments are almost bound, professionally, to be suspicious and afraid of other governments. There is no need for the rest of us to follow that lead. Christians above all should be able to cast aside fear and suspicion. They should also refuse to be excited by false hopes of a stream-lined, chromium-plated material paradise to come next month, and to be depressed and angry when those hopes are disappointed. The secular-minded man, who must put all his eggs in the political basket because he has no other, may well be afraid when he sees how easily they may be broken; and being afraid he is not likely to think wisely. Whatever may happen to our civilization, our institutions, our material means in general, none of which are wholly good, or to our earthly lives in particular, God will not be cheated. Christians should be the best guardians of civilization and political order just because they do not hope too much from them and are not too frightened of losing them.

A. D. RITCHIE

SUBJECT INDEX AND GLOSSARY

Abraham, 146, 216 f.

ABSOLUTE, that which exists by itself without any necessary relationship to any other being.

Acts of the Apostles, reliability of, 227; written by St. Luke, 226.

Adam (and Eve), 47, 148, 212, 214.

AGNOSTIC, one who believes that nothing is known or can be known of God.

Agnosticism, 21 ff.; inconsistency of, 22, 98; cause of, 21, 175 f.

Alternatives to Christianity, 210 f.

Amos, 146.

Andrew, St., 234, 237, 240.

Angels, 141, 229.

Animal soul, 130.

Animals, 130, 166, 214.

APOSTASY, abandonment of religious faith.

Apostles, what became of the, 237 ff.

Apostles' Creed, 26, 37, 146, 194.

Arbitration, 246.

Army, training in the, 196.

ASCETICISM, the practice of severe self-discipline, especially in solitude.

Asceticism, Calvin's, 18.

Astrological superstition, 30 f.

Atheism, 175.

ATHEIST, one who does not believe that God exists.

Atonement, 232.

'Bad', see good.

Baillie, D. M., Where was God when Christ was here?, 77 ff.

Baillie, John, Are not all men agnostics?, 21 ff.; quoted, 234.

'Begotten', difference from 'created', 184.

Behaviour, Christian, 181 ff.

Belief, difficulty in, 96.

Bethlehem, 226.

Bevan, Edwyn, Can you prove that Jesus lived?, 83 ff.

Bible, the, 202; wrong views of, 212 f.; inspiration of, 213.

Bible study, 184 ff.

Bodies, use of, 39 f., 47.

Body and soul, 131.

Body, the resurrection of the, 134 ff., 140, 230.

Brooks, Bishop Phillips, 58.

Buddha, 89, 147, 231.

Bull, Paul, The Virgin Birth, 93 ff.

Bunyan, John, 37.

Caesar, Julius, 231.

Cairns, D. S., What is salvation?, 174 ff.

Calvin, John, 18, 85; on weekly communion, 203.

CATEGORICALLY, without any conditions, absolutely.

Cecil, Lord Hugh, The Resurrection of the Body, 134 ff.

Character, 181 ff., et passim.
 Christian, 234.

Christian standards, 153, 191 ff.
 tradition, 147 f., 195.

Christians, belief of the first, 15, 179; first duty of, 183; persecution of, 229.

Christianity, 15, 176 ff., 181 ff., 183 ff.
 and pacifism, 242 ff.
 as dope, 208.
 has it failed?, 204 ff.
 not fashionable, 186.
 teaching of, 9, 32, 139 ff., 179 f., 181 f., 195.

Christie, J. T., The Men God wants us to be, 181 ff.

Church, the, 86, 129, 179, 194 ff.
 belief in, 194 ff.
 mystical body, 126.
 unity of, 195.

Church attendance, 198 ff., reasons against, 196, 201.
Churches, failure of the, 208 ff.
Churchill, Winston, 85–86, 167.
Citizenship, good, 128.
Civilization, Christian, 247.
Clairvoyance, 139.
COGNITIVE, involving real knowledge, not feeling.
Coleridge, S. T., 198.
Communion, the Holy, 99, 126, 190, 194, 203.
with God, 179 f.
CONATIVE, willing to proceed from conviction to action.
Confession of sin, 196.
Confucius, 89, 147, 181.
CONSECRATION, a setting apart as sacred.
CORRELATION, the bringing of things into relation with each other.
Courage, 5, 181.
Covenant, God's, 217.
'Created', difference from 'begotten', 184.
Creation of man, 214.
Cremation, 140.
Criticism, 'higher', 212 ff.
literary and historical, 219.

Damnation, 49, 155; see Hell.
Dante, 155.
D'Arcy, M. C., In what way is Christ my Saviour?, 123.
Darwin, Charles, 93.
David, King, 29.
Death, 58 ff., 132, 134 ff., 178 f.
life after, 139 ff., 148, 150 ff.
salvation from, 175, 179 f.
DEMONETIZE, deprive of status.
Destiny, Man's, 15, 145 ff., 150 ff., 194.
Devil, the, 48, 49, 150, 156, 229; see also Serpent.
Dewar, Lindsay, Does God notice our prayers?, 65 ff.
Dickie, E. P., Why did Christ work miracles?, 107 ff.

Discipline, 5, 127.
of God, 217.
Dodd, C. H., Did not someone have to betray Jesus?, 101 ff.
Doubting your doubts, 93, 97.
Drinking, 191.
DUALISM, the theory of independent powers of good and evil.
Duncan, George S., Can we believe in the New Testament?, 225 ff.

Earth, end of the, 59.
Easter, 115.
Eden, Garden of, 212.
Ends and means, distinction between, 62.
Enemies, love of, 188 f.
Environment, 127.
Eternal life before Christ, 145 ff.
Eternal punishment, see Hell.
Eternity, 180.
ETHIC, recognized morality or duty.
Eucharist, see Communion, Holy.
Eusebius, 238.
Evil power, 43 ff.
Evil, problem of, 38 ff., 47.
EXPEDIENCY, desirableness.
EXTORTIONATE, oppressive.
EXTRANEOUS, not belonging to.

Faith, 128, 146, 176, 224.
matter of, 113, 114.
unquestioning, 97.
Fall of man, 119 ff., 165 f., 215 f.
Family life, 185.
'Father', key word, 183.
Fear, what to, 153.
Fisher, Archbishop G. F., Why do you believe in God?, 53 ff.
Why do you believe in the Church?, 194 ff.
Forgiveness, 185.
Fortune, belief in, 30.
Frazer, Sir James, quoted, 84.
Free Will, 34, 41, 45, 109, 152.
FUNDAMENTALIST, a maintainer of traditional orthodox beliefs.

Gehenna, description of, 155.
Genesis stories, 214.
Gibbon, Edward, 244.
God, and creation, 41, 44 f., 69, 161.
  and evil, 38 ff., 43, 54.
  and goodness, 162 ff.
  and man, 54, 181 ff.
  and prayer, 65 ff., 69 ff., 73 ff., 160.
  and sin, 162 ff.
  and suffering, 35, 57 ff.
  and temptation, 157 ff.
  association with, 127 ff., 175 ff.
  belief in, 53 ff.
  concern with the Jews, 217.
  definition of, 26, 33, 43, 70, 73.
  desire for man, 181, 206.
  Fatherhood of, 174, 185.
  grace of, 153, 177 f., 191, 196.
  guidance of, 61 ff.
  Hebrew conception of, 29.
  intervention of, 99.
  justice of, 156.
  love for, 129.
  love of, 60, 71, 129, 141, 144, 150, 153, 155 f., 180, 188.
  mercy of, 156.
  New Testament conception of, 31, 231.
  omnipotence of, 32, 134.
  omnipresence of, 69 ff., 79 ff., 177.
  power of, 139.
  purpose of, 64, 67, 134 f., 148 f., 206.
  self-limitation of, 33.
  trust in, 56.
  who made?, 26 ff.
  will not be cheated, 247.
  wrath of, 150.
'Good', definition of, 44, 163.
Good and bad, 38 f., 43 ff., 162 ff.
Goodness, wrong idea of, 181 ff.
Gore, Bishop Charles, 93.
Gospel, message of the, 15, 105, 176 f., 218.
  St. Paul and the simple, 232 ff.

Gospels, the, date of, 227.
  differences in, 218 ff.
  earliest, 219, 227.
  how written, 228.
  reliability of, 225 ff.
  why four, 218.
Grace, 153, 165, 173, 177 f., 191, 196, 235.
  means of, 184.
Greco-Roman view of the gods, 30.
Grensted, L. W., *How could Christ pray?*, 73.
Guidance, definition of, 61.

Habits, 199 f.
Hankey, Donald, 10.
Happiness, 36, 57.
Heaven, 80 ff., 141 f., 145 ff., 150 ff.
Hebert, A. G., *What are we to make of the Old Testament?*, 212 ff.
Hebrew conception of God, 24.
Hegesippus, 238.
Hell, 49, 142 f., 150 ff., 155 f., 229 f. descent into, 146.
Henry, Matthew, 199.
Herbert, George, 199.
HERESY, an opinion contrary to the doctrine of the Church.
HIGHER CRITICISM, historical research and judgement applied to the Bible, 212 ff.
Historic facts, St. Paul and, 234.
History, centres on Jesus Christ, 205.
  Bible starts, 216.
Holy Spirit, *see* Spirit.
Humanism, 19.
Huxley, T. H., invents term 'agonistic', 22.
Hypocrisy, definition of, 18.

Idols, 27.
IMMANENT, permanently pervading.
Immortality, 139 ff., not necessarily universal, 148.
Incarnation, *see* Jesus Christ.

INCORPOREAL, not composed of matter.

Inge, W. R., *Leading a Christian Life*, 15 ff.

INTEGRATING, making up as a whole.

Israel, Israelites, 216 f.

James, St., 65, 103, 233, 238, 240.
Liturgy of, 99.

James, M. R., *What became of the Apostles?*, 237 ff.

Jeans, Sir James, 59.

Jerusalem, 226; fall of, 217.

Jesus Christ, 87 ff., 157 ff., 204 ff., 225 ff.
and economic disputes, 17.
and God, 15, 28, 54, 72, 73 ff., 77 ff., 88 f., 147 ff., 194, 225 f., 231.
and miracles, 107 ff., 229 f.
and money-grubbing, 16.
and prayer, 73 ff.
and St. Paul, 232.
and society, 17.
and Sunday, 200 f.
and temptation, 73, 110, 158 ff., 229.
and the Church, 126, 194 ff., 199 f.
as Judge, 142.
as Messiah, 217.
as Saviour, 123 ff., 146.
as the Sower, 207.
betrayal of, 101 ff.
boyhood of, 10.
challenge of, 25.
content of His Revelation, 15, 76, 87 ff., 176 f.
crucifixion, 66, 101 ff., 225.
enemies of, 207.
friends of, 207 f.
gospel story of, 218 ff.
historic proof of, 83 ff., 225.
imitation of, 189 f.
Incarnation of, 57, 73, 79 ff., 93 ff., 126, 147 ff., 178.
love of, 71, 140.
purges temple, 221.

resurrection of, 54, 57, 90 f., 94, 114 ff., 135 f., 139 ff., 202, 225 f., 230.
risen body of, 135.
standard of values, 16, 17, 182, 191.
the centre of history, 205.
the Spirit of, 127.
the 'Word', 147.
traditions of, 219.
union with, 93, 125.
virgin birth of, 93 ff., 230.
what He hated, 18.

John, St., 103, 136, 184, 219 ff., 237, 239; quoted, 147.

Judas Iscariot, 237; the character of, 103, 151.

Justification, 232, 234 ff.

Kant, Immanuel, 35.

Keats, John, quoted, 132.

Kelman, Dr. John, 174.

Kelvin, Lord, 109.

Kirk, Bishop K. E., *What is the Holy Spirit?*, 127 ff.

Knox, Mgr. Ronald A., *Why does God make sin so easy?*, 162 ff.

Legends, 90; apocryphal, 228.

Leighton, Sir Gerald, 95.

Lewis, C. S., *What are we to make of Christ?*, 87 ff.

LIBERAL, tending to subordinate tradition to harmony with modern thought.

'Life' means soul, 130.

Life after death, 139 ff., 145 ff.
mystery of, 21.

Loaves and fishes, miracle of, 229.

Lord's Day, 198; *see also* Sunday.

Lord's Prayer, 75, 157 ff., 185.

Love, definition of, 188.
Christian, 16, 62, 72, 129, 188 ff.
falling in, 167.
the Gospel of, 17.

LOWER CRITICISM, research and judgement to establish the correct text of the Bible in manuscripts, &c.; not concerned with historical interpretation.

Luck, belief in, 30.

Luke, St., Gospel of, 219 ff.; author of Acts, 226, 237.

Luther, M.. 85.

McCormick, Pat, 'Life after death', 139 ff.

MACHIAVELLIAN, unscrupulous in political affairs, 209.

Mackintosh, H. R., *Who made God?*, 10, 26 ff.

MacLeod, Sir George F., *Is the story of the Resurrection true?*, 114 ff.

Macmurray, John, *Isn't Christianity played out?*, 204 ff.

Man, and God, 54 f., 164 f., 181 ff., 194, 206.
  destiny of, 153.
  fall of, 49, 119 ff., 165, 215.
  magnanimous, character of, 182.
  nature of, 41 f., 45, 101, 130 f., 181 ff.
  Old Testament story of creation of, 214 ff.
  rebellion of, 46, 215.
  spirit of, 133.

Manichaean heresy, 156.

Manson, T. W., *Would God lead us into temptation?*, 157.

Mark, St., Gospel of, 218 ff.; the earliest, 219, 227.

Marriage, 50 f., 129, 191.

Mars, 30.

Martindale, C. C., *If God made everything, who made evil?*, 38.

Mary, the Blessed Virgin, 97, 230.

Matthew, St., 237; Gospel of, 218.

Matthews, W. R., *How do the consciences of Christians differ?*, 61.

Maxwell, W. D., *Does a Christian need to go to Church?*, 198.

Memory, the oriental, 220.

Mendelians, 95.

Messiah, 217; *see also* Jesus.

Meyer, Eduard, 84.

Micklem, N., *Eternal life for those before Christ?*, 145 ff.

Mill, J. S., 33.

Milne, A. A., 198.

Milton, John, 155.

Miracles, 107 ff., 229 f., of the Resurrection, 114 ff., 230.

Mohammed, 85; and Christ, 89.

Moore, R. W., *Why is it wrong to do wrong?*, 169.

Moral improvement, 17.

Morality, present standard of, 19.

'Natural', definition of, 99.

Natural religion, 98.

Nazareth, 226.

Nazi Germany, 169, 243.

Nero, persecution under, 239.

New Testament, and the Apostles, 237.
  conception of God, 31 ff.
  message of 217, 218 ff.
  trustworthiness of, 225.

Nietzsche, F., 207.

Obedience, 176, 189 f.

OBSCURANTISM, opposition to inquiry or reform.

Offences, technical, 169.

Old Testament, 212 ff.; saints, 145.

Omnipotence of God, 69 ff., 79 ff., 177.

Omnipresence of God, 32, 134.

Pacifists, Christian, 242 f.

Papias, 238.

Parents, 65; respect for, 150.

Paul, St., 207, 226, 239.
  and the 'simple Gospel', 232 ff.
  on Christ's death, 189.
  on the Christian life, 15, 19, 36, 128, 133, 153.
  on God, 32, 42.
  on the resurrection of the body, 135 ff., 140, 142.
  other quotations, 69, 98, 217.

Peace, 128, 242 ff.

Perfect, on being, 187 ff.

Personality, 134.

Peter, St., 60, 103, 104, 204, 218, 233, 237.
  at Rome, 239.
  1st Epistle of, 146.

Pilate, Pontius, 225; character of, 102, 104.

PLAGIARIZE, to use another person's thoughts or writings as one's own.

Plato, 19, 90, 101, 146, 181.

Police force, international, 246.

Politics, Christian attitude to, 19, 40.

POLYTHEISTIC, having many gods.

POSTULATE, to claim or take for granted.

POTENTIAL, existing as a possibility.

Power, evil, 43 ff.

Prayer, 65 ff., 69 ff., 157 ff., 190, 199; see also Lord's Prayer.

PREDESTINED, Fate appointed from the beginning.

PREMISS, a basis of reasoning.

Priggishness, 181, 191.

Prodigal Son, the, 185.

Proof, forms of, 83.

Psalms, Book of, 21.

PSEUDO-, false or counterfeit.

Psychical Research, Society for, 131.

Pump, Mr., 198.

Punishment, 142, 150 ff.

Quickswood, Lord, see Cecil, Lord Hugh.

Ramsay, Sir William, 227.

Raven, C. E., Can God watch over everyone at once?, 69 ff.

Read, D. H. C., What do you mean by the Fall of man?, 119 ff.

Reason, not enough, 98.

Redemption, the, 123 ff., 165, 206 f.

REGRESS, working back in thought from one thing to another.

Religion, begins with God, 186.
  of the inarticulate, 10.

RENASCENCE, rebirth or renewal.

Repentance, 153.

REPUDIATE, to disown or reject.

Resurrection, Christian idea of, 139.
  of the body, 134 ff., 140 ff.
  of Christ, 54, 57, 90, 94, 114 ff.

Revelation, Book of, 229.

Reverence, 35.

Rewards and punishments, future, 142.

Right and wrong, 38 ff., 53 f., 169 ff.

Ritchie, A. D. Shouldn't all Christians be pacifists?, 242 ff.

Roman world, religion of, 30.

Romanes, George, 93, 98.

Russell, Bertrand, 74.

Sabbath, the, 200 ff.

Sacraments, 184 f.

Saints, Old Testament, 145.

Salvation, 146, 153; definition of, 174 ff., 232.

Satan, see Devil, the.

Sayers, D. L., Is there an evil power?, 43.

SCEPTIC, one who doubts, in contrast to those who believe.

Science, 19, 28, 53, 96, 108, 139.
  and faith, 114.

Security against war, 246.

Selfishness, 150.

Self-limitation of God, 33.

Sermons, 202.

Serpent, the, 215.

Sex, 50, 94 ff.

Shakespeare, William, 21, 84.

Shaw, G. Bernard, 85–86.

Sin, 44, 151, 155, 162 ff., 173, 175, 185, 189, 196, 206.
  original, 189.
  unforgivable, 155.

Slim, Field-Marshal, 5.

Smoking, 191.

Society, founded on trust, 171.

Socrates, 231.

Sodom, the men of, 216.
Sorley, W. R., *What is the Soul?*, 130 ff.
Soul, 130 ff., 148.
Spencer, Herbert, 23.
Spirit, the Holy, 127 ff., 139, 178, 217.
  fruits of the, 128.
Spiritualism, 139.
Stars, superstitious belief in, 31.
Stewart, James S., *Did St. Paul spoil the simple Gospel?*, 232 ff.
Stoicism, 16, 183.
SUBJECTIVE, depending on personal point of view.
Suffering, 16, 35, 57.
Sunday, Christian use of, 200 ff.
Supernatural, the, 99.
Superstition, 30 ff., 108.
Survival, not same as resurrection, 139.
Suspicion, 247.
Sympathy, 16.
SYNONYMOUS, exactly the same as.
Syrian Church, Gospel of the, 218.

Tacitus, on Jesus, 225.
Talents, parable of the, 142.
Tatian, 218.
Taylor, A. E., *Is God really almighty?*, 29 ff.
Technical offences, 169, 172.
Temple, purging of the, 221.
Temptation, 157 ff.
Testament, *see* Old *and* New Testaments.
THEIST, one who believes in the existence of a god or gods in the most general sense.
Thomas, St., 136, 137.
  Apocryphal Gospel of, 228.
  in India, 240.
Thornton, L. S., *Is there such a place as hell?*, 150 ff.
Thugs, 243.
Tongues, speaking with, 229.
TOTALITARIAN, a polity which permits of no rival loyalties or parties.

Tradition, the Christian, 147.
TRANSCENDENT, excelling, surpassing.
Trinity, the Holy, 73, 98.
Trust, in God, 56.
  society founded on, 171.
Truth, 139.
  definition and meaning of, 229.
  spiritual, 114.

Unforgivable sin, 155.
Universe, meaning of the, 177.
  creation of the, 212.
Unknowable, the, 23.
UTOPIAN, fanciful.

'Vale of soul-making', 132.
VALID, sound.
VENDETTA, pursuit of revenge which keeps a quarrel perpetually alive.
VICISSITUDES, changes.
V.I.P., Very important person.
Virgin Birth, the, 93 ff.
VIRTUAL, really though not actually.
VITALIZING, giving life to.
VOLITION, power of willing.

War, 35.
  blessed by the Church, 209.
  Christianity and, 242 ff.
  First World, 245.
  just, 245.
  Second World, 245.
Webb, C. C. J., *How can we be like Christ?*, 187 ff.
Westminster Directory, the, 203.
Whately, Archbishop R., 83.
Will, free, 34.
Wind, Holy Spirit compared to the, 128.
Winnington-Ingram, A. F., *Is hell reconcilable with love?*, 155 f.
World, soul and the, 132.
'World-rulers', 31 f.
Worry, 17.
Worship, open air, 199.
Wrong, Why is it wrong to do?, 155 ff.